RESISTING THE BONHOEFFER BRAND

Resisting the Bonhoeffer Brand

A Life Reconsidered

CHARLES MARSH

CASCADE *Books* · Eugene, Oregon

RESISTING THE BONHOEFFER BRAND
A Life Reconsidered

Cascade Books
An Imprint of Wipf and Stock Publishers
199 W. 8th Ave., Suite 3
Eugene, OR 97401

www.wipfandstock.com

PAPERBACK ISBN: 978-1-6667-3089-0
HARDCOVER ISBN: 978-1-6667-2291-8
EBOOK ISBN: 978-1-6667-2292-5

Cataloguing-in-Publication data:

Names: Marsh, Charles, 1958–, author.

Title: Resisting the Bonhoeffer brand : a life reconsidered / Charles Marsh.

Description: Eugene, OR: Cascade Books, 2023 | Includes bibliographical references and index.

Identifiers: ISBN 978-1-6667-3089-0 (paperback) | ISBN 978-1-6667-2291-8 (hardcover) | ISBN 978-1-6667-2292-5 (ebook)

Subjects: LCSH: Bonhoeffer, Dietrich, 1906–1945. | Marsh, Charles, 1958–. Strange glory.

Classification: BX4827.B57 M37 2023 (print) | BX4827.B57 (ebook)

JANUARY 17, 2023 1:01 PM

For John W. de Gruchy, whose theological life illumines
the path from the phraseological to the real.

The biographer truly succeeds if a distinct literary form can be found for the particular life.

—LEON EDEL, *WRITING LIVES*

WRITING LIVES

"My God, how does one write a biography?" asks Virginia Woolf, as she muscles her way into a life of her friend, the artist and critic Roger Fry. "How can one make a life out of six cardboard boxes full of tailor's bills, love letters and old picture postcards?"[1]

The only way forward, Woolf resolves, is to proceed like the miner's canary, "testing the atmosphere, detecting falsity, unreality, and the presence of obsolete conventions," searching from all this variety for narrative unity. "Writing lives is the devil!" she concedes.[2]

John Updike once quipped that most biographies are "just novels with indexes." And he's correct insofar as writing biography is a literary endeavor that brings imaginative powers to bear on place, character, ideation, and plot. Unlike fiction, however, biography searches for truth in lived lives. It cannot shirk its responsibility to history. The biographer is sustained by "the near missionary drive to save, if not a soul then a personality, for the company of future generations."[3] In her book *Body Parts*, the biographer Hermione Lee, who has written on figures such as Virginia

---

1. Woolf to Roger Fry, in *The Letters of Virginia Woolf: 1936–1941*, ed. Nigel Nicolson and Joanne Trautmann (New York: Harcourt Brace Jovanovich, 1975) 6:226, 374.

2. Woolf, "The Art of Biography," in *Collected Essays*, ed. Leonard Woolf (London: Chatto and Windus, 1959 [1925]) 4:226; and Woolf, *Letters*, 6:245.

3. John Updike cited in Hermione Lee, *Biography: A Short Introduction* (New York: Oxford University Press, 2009) 7; and Marc Pachter, "The Biographer Himself: An Introduction," in *Telling Lives: The Biographer's Art*, ed. Marc Pachter (Washington, DC: New Republic, 1979) 4.

Woolf, Edith Wharton, Penelope Fitzgerald, and Philip Roth, likens her work to a ferrier moving between the dead and the living, until a likeness of a lived life is achieved. Her challenge, she explains, is to probe beneath the public, polished self and uncover the biographical wires—between layers of complexity and stupendous detail—whose spark brings a person to life.[4] To write a life is to make that life vivid and credible.

WRITING *STRANGE GLORY*: A LIFE OF DIETRICH BONHOEFFER

I began work on *Strange Glory* in the spring semester of 2007 while on research leave in Berlin. I made my first trip to the Staatsbibliothek, the capacious city library designed by Hans Scharoun near the Postdamer Platz, after gaining access to the Dietrich Bonhoeffer archives, recently obtained from the estate of Eberhard and Renate Bethge. Most of the documents in these bankers' boxes would appear—if they had not already—in the sixteen-volume *Dietrich Bonhoeffer Works* that would contain every morsel of Bonhoeffer's written life, with a one-volume index and other volumes likely to appear as new papers came to light.[5]

4. Lee, *Biography*, 2. As a counterpoint, Wolfe's biography of Fry, published in 1940, would be widely considered the worst book she ever wrote, "despite the fact that she had known him and his circle intimately through his sister Vanessa. Concerned not to upset Fry's widow, or scandalize society, or run into legal difficulties, she found herself unable to portray the real Frye—a problem she never faced in her fiction her private correspondence or her diary where she positively reveled in the securing of personalities and their reputations" (Nigel Hamilton, *Biography: A Brief History* [Cambridge, MA: Harvard University Press, 2007] 162).

5. "Of value to those who want or need the whole dossier," Elisabeth Sifton and Fritz Stern surmise, "the enterprise has the weakness of all such unwieldy monuments: its close-up attention to every detail, its assiduous editorial apparatus, repeatedly adjusted and updated, seem to us to ascribe to Bonhoeffer more significance than may be appropriate, the implicit presumption being that everything he did was important, everything he wrote worthy of preservation. Bonhoeffer himself never claimed this" (Sifton and Stern, *No Ordinary Men: Dietrich Bonhoeffer and Hans von Dohnanyi, Resisters Against Hitler in Church and State* [New York: New York Review Books Collections, 2013] 145).

The singularities of Bonhoeffer's life, evidence of which I held in my hands (sleeved in archival gloves) revealed an altogether different image of the man whose philosophical theology had been the subject of my doctoral dissertation twenty-five years earlier. Registration papers for a new Audi convertible, a bank slip from the joint account he shared with Eberhard, files on race relations in the United States, inventories of his wardrobe and library, austere landscape photographs of North Africa, Polaroids of Bonhoeffer and Eberhard making funny faces and goofing around on the Baltic seaboard, postcards from Texas, a brief correspondence with Mahatma Gandhi—all parts of a mosaic. Who is this person? How I can work with this material to give proof of life?

I felt further the gentle nudge into biography.

It is a remarkable story. By the age of twenty-one, this golden child of the Berlin Grunewald had already written a doctoral dissertation that would be hailed by Karl Barth as a "theological miracle." He completed a second dissertation by the age of twenty-five. But he wasn't content in the library. Unusual for a German scholar of his generation, he felt an uncommon hunger to see new places and to experience life beyond his native land; he would travel widely and whenever possible. Between 1924 and 1932, he journeyed to Italy and Libya; to Spain, France, and Morocco; to Cuba and Mexico. He road-tripped through the Jim Crow South and spent an intense six months immersed in the community of Harlem. His experiences and encounters during these travels challenged Bonhoeffer to reexamine his vocation as theologian and pastor and his notions of citizenship and patriotism, to embark upon what he would call "the turning from the phraseological to the real."[6] This attention to the real served him well as the exhilarating and often languorous years of study and travel during the 1920s opened onto a horrible new decade.

In the decades since he was executed on Adolf Hitler's orders for the crime of high treason in the concentration camp in Flossenbürg, Bonhoeffer has become one of the most widely read and

---

6. Barth and Bonhoeffer quoted in Marsh, *Strange Glory: A Life of Dietrich Bonhoeffer* (New York: Knopf, 2014) 57, 125.

influential religious thinkers of our time. His life and legacy have inspired millions of women and men to live and to think out of "a higher satisfaction," which is to say, as Bonhoeffer would write, "with an eye on the coming generation spirited by the excellences of Christ." Indeed, "what remains for us is only the very narrow path," he wrote in a letter to his family on New Year's Eve 1942, "sometimes barely discernible, of taking each day as if it were the last and yet living it faithfully and responsibly as if there were yet to be a great future. . . . That is the course that has, in practice, been forced upon us."[7]

His more popular works make biblical faith intelligible to believers and nonbelievers alike, never reducing difficult ideas to clichés. Few other modern theologians cross so many boundaries while remaining exuberantly and—one should add—generously Christian. His story unites religious liberals and evangelicals; Catholics and Protestants; Christians, Jews, and Muslims; and mystics, idealists, and activists in shared admiration of an indisputably authentic witness. For Bonhoeffer, bravery in the face of danger, intellectual curiosity, and a cosmopolitan outlook are the highest virtues. Bonhoeffer was the rare intellectual who reconciled the pursuits of beauty and passion with courage and justice.

From the start, Bonhoeffer insisted that the essence of Christianity was not its abstract precepts but the concrete reality of lived faith. Following Hitler's appointment as Reich Chancellor in 1933, the German church was soon Nazified, along with every other state-sponsored institution, but it was the Nuremberg laws that set Bonhoeffer's earthly life on a collision course with the führer. His denunciation of the race statues as heresy and his insistence on the church's moral obligation to defend all victims of state violence, regardless of race or religion, alienated him from what would become the Reich church and even many fellow church dissidents. Bonhoeffer would find himself a voice crying in the wilderness,

---

7. Bonhoeffer, *Dietrich Bonhoeffer Works: Letters and Papers from Prison*, trans. Lisa E. Dahill et al., readers ed. (Minneapolis: Fortress, 2015) 8:50. Hereafter, *Dietrich Bonhoeffer Works* is abbreviated *DBWE*.

until, finally, he understood that true moral responsibility obliged him to treason, a trajectory for which he would pay with his life.

The biographer feasts upon the singularities of lived experience. If we learn that Albert Camus liked to play Ping-Pong and had a cat named Cigarette, that George Washington had bad teeth and big feet, or that Janis Joplin joined the Future Nurses of America Club in high school, we may not be edified, but we are, as Catherine Drinker Bowen says, "warmed to the presence of a living being; we are less worshipful perhaps and more intrigued."[8] The Ping-Pong and the cat are how you tell a good story.

All evidence of a life is stirred into this rich gumbo of a genre. Tempting as it may be to create scenes and conversations out of pure imagination—Edmund Morris gave us an entirely fictitious character in his *Dutch: A Memoir of Ronald Reagan*, indeed a doppelgänger who penned the memoir—the biographer cleaves to the materials of lives lived. As Leon Edel writes, "Biography is a record, in words, of something that is as mercurial and as flowing, as compact of temperament and emotion, as the human spirit itself."[9] To which I would add that biography is memory of particular bodies committed to narrative.

I'd written short biographical narratives, stories of what Virginia Woolf called "obscure lives," in my books on the civil rights movement.[10] My initial plan for the Bonhoeffer book was to frame his theological awakening in the context of his two visits to the United States. I would expand the ten-thousand-word format to forty thousand words; otherwise, I'd follow the same process I'd followed when writing short. But it soon became clear that to write about Bonhoeffer in America was to write about Bonhoeffer

8. Holly George-Warren, *Janis: Her Life and Music* (New York: Simon & Schuster, 2019) 9; Bowen cited in Pachter, "Biographer Himself," 2.

9. Edel, *Writing Lives: Principia Biographica* (New York: Norton, 1984) 33.

10. Woolf cited in Lee, *Biography*, 140. Also, see Woolf, "Lives of the Obscure," in *The Essays of Virginia Woolf*, vol. 4, ed. Andrew McNeillie (London: Hogarth, 1994).

in Germany, and to write about Bonhoeffer the theologian was to write about Bonhoeffer the friend; this would be longer than a long essay or a brief life.

Some biographers start with a structure in mind. I was drawn to a slideshow of scenes, like reels in the View-Master stereoscope. I was drawn to persistent images and words. I would later understand this to be a common process. You start with a sentence or image, not a concept or thesis, and then trust that over time you'll see and hear the story. Indeed, the novelist Robert Stone once said that time is the writer's only commodity, but I think the writer's commodity is trust. "You write the book that your education, your temperament, your training, your class, your race, your gender, your nationality incline you toward. You can't write a book as another person," Lee explained in a *Paris Review* interview.[11]

And so I kept a box for each of the fourteen chapters. I filled notebooks with sketches, words, and phrases. I taped maps and photos and index cards on my office wall. Then, when I started writing, I monitored my word count obsessively. And I wrote three hundred words a day, even on days when I knew I'd delete most of them. I'm always asking writers about their process because I wish I had a better one. But no tweak in the daily routine can make writing easy.

I knew enough about storytelling to appreciate a sense of place. Bonhoeffer also pondered the geographic influences on Christian faith and practice. In a letter written during his year as an assistant vicar in Barcelona, he allowed that his understanding of dogmatics had been "unsettled" by the strong impressions of Mediterranean culture. "It's still difficult to articulate these impressions," he writes. "In any case I now do have serious questions whether Barth could have written in Spain—whether he had any understanding at all for circumstances outside Germany."[12]

11. Lee, interview by Louisa Thomas, "The Art of Biography No. 4," *Paris Review* 205 (Summer 2013) https://www.theparisreview.org/interviews/6231/the-art-of-biography-no-4-hermione-lee.

12. Bonhoeffer to Walter Dreß, March 13, [19]28, in *DBWE: Barcelona, Berlin, New York 1928–1931*, ed. Clifford J. Green (Minneapolis: Fortress, 2007) 10:76.

I journeyed—*auf den Spuren von Bonhoeffer*—to the places he lived or visited: Wrocław, Poland (Breslau); Tübingen; Rome; Paris; the Baltic seaboard and the Pomeranian plains; Barcelona; London; Stockholm; Copenhagen; New York; Geneva, Ettal; Prague; Friedrichsbrunn in the eastern Harz Mountains; and the village and concentration camp of Flossenbürg, where Bonhoeffer was executed on April 9, 1945. When circumstances forced me to cancel a trip to Tripoli and Tétouan, I read passages from Paul Bowles's *Under the Sheltering Sky* to get a feel for Morocco. I was always happy to return to Berlin, but I tried to embrace Bonhoeffer's unwavering spirit of exploring new lands and cultures.

According to the protocols of the Bonhoeffer guild, you tell the story by adhering to the master narrative of Eberhard Bethge, whose 1969 account remains the one acceptable touchstone for writing Bonhoeffer's life. Philip Ziegler, a Christian ethicist who brings a sharp analytical mind to Bonhoeffer studies, makes this point in a review of Ferdinand Schlingensiepen's 2007 biography: "The study is dependent upon Eberhard Bethge's biography, as all later tellings of Bonhoeffer's life must be." I generally agree with Ziegler, though I would add that all later tellings of Bonhoeffer must also go their own way. In Schlingensiepen's view, however, any credible biographer must adhere to Bethge's narrative structure as delineated by three major periods: (1) The Lure of Theology, 1906–31; (2) The Cost of Being a Christian, 1931–40; and (3) Sharing Germany's Destiny, 1940–45.

My approach was to portray Bonhoeffer in his singular complexity, which is to say, his strange glory. With regard to the nature of his relationship with Eberhard—discussed in detail later in this book—that meant making space over four chapters for the careful revealing of evidence. This approach was the fruit of conversations with colleagues, friends, and writers but was most significantly influenced by the appearance of the *Dietrich Bonhoeffer Works*, especially volume 16, *Conspiracy and Imprisonment*, pages 80–164.[13] I consider it one of my life's great joys to have known Eberhard as

---

13. Fortress Press published the English-language translation of volume 16 in 2006.

a colleague and mentor. I knew him to be always generous, open, and free. I do not think he would feel threatened by my portrayal; in fact, I think he would have been intrigued to see a younger theologian, enraptured by Bonhoeffer's life and thought, wrestle his best friend free of a monochromatic narrative. I am quite sure he would not have cast aspersions on my integrity for examining aspects of character long ignored.

THEOLOGY AND BIOGRAPHY

At the level of craft, telling a theological life should be no different than telling any other kind of life. Every good biographer maintains the desire to save a personality from the clutch of familiarity. The challenge is in determining how to enlist the tenets of belief in service to story. The infinite does not appear in the dramatis personae; instead, theologians enumerate transcendence under the terms of specific doctrinal commitments. It may be said of the theological biography that it tells a life out of a "higher satisfaction," but this should not be taken as a method or dogma.[14] The theological biographer writes with the hope of rendering the character's faith as a vivid and credible element of the story. Otherwise, I feel rather agnostic toward the idea of a theological biography.

Biographies written about theologians make up a modest canon. Theologians writing biographies about other theologians— take a moment to make a list—make up an even smaller canon. After a quick look in my library, I can count ten. Biography inconveniences dogma. Theological reflection is not well-suited to the

14. Bonhoeffer, *Letters and Papers*, 52. Writing out of a higher satisfaction is not a method or approach; it's a way of writing lives that enables the reader to see in the narrative, as through a glass faintly, openings to divinity. Writing against the horizon of eternity—to risk a phrase that may terribly mislead—is the only "contract for services rendered" in theological biography that differs from other types and which "operates," I think, "slightly differently" than in biographies of nonreligious persons (see Marsh, "Introduction—Lived Theology: Method, Style, and Pedagogy," in *Lived Theology: New Perspectives on Method, Style, and Pedagogy*, eds. Charles Marsh et al. [New York: Oxford University Press, 2016] 1–20).

task of excavating the truth of a particular life; discerning the idiosyncrasies that form a life requires a certain bracketing of doctrine (e.g., God, the Trinity, the divine, the church, the holy). Moreover, theologians are not generally inclined to tell secrets. We'll happily take on the Big Questions but not so much our own misbehavior.

Wilhelm Pauck abandoned his biography of his friend Paul Tillich, I've been told, because he said he couldn't make sense of the Schelling. But it's more likely that Tillich's extramarital affairs and rumored sexual advances to students presented an insurmountable challenge.

Ferdinand Schlingensiepen—whose criticism of *Strange Glory* I discuss later in this work—may think it's clever to call my biography a novel (*Roman*). Too much character, it would seem, and not enough attention to the inner workings of the "Deutsche Evangelische Kirche and its 28 Landeskirchen."[15] Biography is built on historical reality, of course, but its purpose is finding the truth in the life. This does not mean finding the authentic or essential self but the patterns and manners, "the doubts and vulnerabilities, ambitions and private satisfactions that are hidden within the social personality."[16]

Scholars, pastors, and students routinely enlist Bonhoeffer as an example of how a theologian's ideas are best understood in the context of "lived life."[17] But the way this plays out in most critical studies is by treating his life as a placeholder for his thought. Decades of theological engagement with Bonhoeffer have produced

15. Ferdinand Schlingensiepen and Heiner Süselbeck, "Amerikanische Biografien vereinnahmen Bonhoeffer. Ein Blick auf Charles Marsh: A Life of Dietrich Bonhoeffer - mit einem Seitenblick auf dasgegensätzliche Buch von Eric Metaxas," International Bonhoeffer Society, n.d. A version of this essay appeared in the International Bonhoeffer Group Rundbrief in 2014, and a modified version of this essay was published in English as Ferdinand Schlingensiepen, "Making Assumptions about Dietrich: How Bonhoeffer Was Made Fit for America," Bonhoeffer Center, n.d., https://www.thebonhoeffercenter. org/index.php?option=com_content&view=article&id=37:schlingensiepen-on-metaxas-and-marsh&catid=21&Itemid=263.

16. Pachter, "Biographer Himself," 10.

17. Jürgen Moltmann, *The Spirit of Life: A Universal Affirmation*, trans. Margaret Kohl (Minneapolis: Fortress, 2001) 183.

mostly one-dimensional biographical accounts.[18] His life is made a compendium of theological insights and historical events.

In a lecture some years ago to my Bonhoeffer seminar, the scholar Victoria Barnett made an interesting remark on the difference between doing historical research and writing biography. She said that after serving as the general editor of the sixteen-volume *Dietrich Bonhoeffer Works*, translating thousands of pages of his writings into English, editing and translating critical and historical studies of Bonhoeffer and the German church crisis, and producing the unabridged English translation of Eberhard Bethge's 1,048-page masterwork, she still didn't have a clear sense of who he was, as a person or a character.

Biography came to me as a quest to capture what Hermione Lee describes as "the 'vital spark' of the human subject."[19] To readers familiar with Bonhoeffer's story, I wanted to create a sense of discovery so that they could encounter him as if for the first time, encounter him in his strange glory. For those unfamiliar with Bonhoeffer, I wanted to do all the things biographers hope for when they write well: approximate in narrative nonfiction "the presence of recognizable, approachable life . . . to catch the special gleam of character."[20]

With regard to his soulmate, Eberhard, I sought to portray their seven-year friendship as a natural unfolding of affection and longing, even if that approach risked seeming at times maddeningly coy. Cleaving to published writings and archives, my initial speculations about how to shape Bonhoeffer's life were at times foiled by the historical record. For example, when I came upon

18. In contrast, literary efforts that made a valiant effort to do justice to Bonhoeffer's complexity have been ignored or even maligned. In particular, Mary Bosanquet's early biography, *The Life and Death of Dietrich Bonhoeffer*, and Denise Giardina's excellent novel *Saints and Villains* were subject to harsh criticism. See John A. Phillips, "Bonhoeffer," *CrossCurrents* 20.1 (1970) 103–5; and Paul Baumann, "Executioner's Song," *New York Times*, April 19, 2008, https://movies2.nytimes.com/books/98/04/19/reviews/980419.19baumant.html.

19. Lee, *Biography*, 3.

20. Pachter, "Biographer Himself," 4.

this line written from the village of Ettal, "I am still a guest here after all."[21] Alas—as the context of the line makes clear—Bonhoeffer said he did not participate in the Eucharist in the Roman Mass in the Benedictine monastery, where he'd found refuge.[22] I wanted very much to show him receiving the host; the monks had treated him like a brother, and such dramatic ecumenism would have fit nicely in the events of 1940–1941 as I narrated them. But the evidence proved otherwise.

HOW FIERCELY HE RAGES

My biography, *Strange Glory*, was published in May 2014 by Knopf/Random House. Throughout the spring and summer, I crisscrossed the country on a book tour, and each event reminded me of the power and reach of Bonhoeffer's story.

Reviewers who found mistakes, errors of fact, incomplete footnotes, or typos in the book sometimes included their observations in their published pieces, though most often they sent a note to my editor or me. Corrections would then be made in new printings. Sometimes readers wrote to share stories of their encounters with Bonhoeffer's thought or to ask questions. I receive all these as acts of kindness, even when they sting.

Responding to a review of *Strange Glory* that appeared in the *New York Times*, an esteemed biographer of W. H. Auden wrote to me with kind words and a clarification about a scene in the book. I'd written that during his tumultuous six-week visit to New York City in the summer of 1939, Bonhoeffer had met the famous poet. The Auden scholar wanted to know my source because the famous poet was a thousand miles away from Manhattan in July 1939. It took me a few days to recall that I'd read the story in Eberhard Bethge's biography: "During this period Bonhoeffer also spoke with the English writer W. H. Auden, who wrote the poem

21. Bonhoeffer to Eberhard Bethge, Ettal, November 23, 1940, in *DBWE: Conspiracy and Imprisonment 1940–1945*, ed. Mark S. Brocker (Minneapolis, MN: Fortress, 2006) 16:89.

22. He boarded at the nearby Hotel Ludwig de Bayer.

'Friday's Child.'"[23] Perhaps Bethge was referring to a phone call or a written exchange, but Bethge died in March 2000 at the age of ninety; otherwise, I would have asked the dear man myself. Still, I'm left wondering why Auden made an appearance in his definitive account.

After the war, Auden wrote a poem about Bonhoeffer called "Friday's Child," but there are no clues in these lines. Although Auden lived in Berlin some ten months between 1928 and 1930, you would not want to speculate in biography on a possible meeting of the two then. In January 1939, Auden moved to New York; he boarded for two months at the George Washington Hotel on 23rd St and Lexington and then took an apartment on the Upper East Side. During Bonhoeffer's six weeks in the city that summer, Auden was traveling with Chester Kallman—Auden had fallen in love with Kallman, and as Josie Holford wrote, "regarded their relationship as a marriage." Acccording to Mendelson, Christoph von Dohanyi would have been mistaken if (as Bethge so reports) he had said "that Auden told him he had met Bonhoeffer in June or July 1939. Perhaps Auden said that the Niebuhrs had told him about Bonhoeffer when Auden met them in 1940; but that's only a far-fetched guess."[24]

This would have all made for fascinating exploration in a work of historical fiction; alas, the "writer of lives," Leon Edel reminds us, "is allowed the imagination of form but not of fact."[25]

Some of the livelier criticism of the book clustered around my narration of Bonhoeffer's sexuality and his relationship with Eberhard Bethge, to which I'll turn later in this book. It's worth noting now that the response to this controversy, long discussed offstage by Bonhoeffer scholars, does not fall along predictable

23. Bethge, *Dietrich Bonhoeffer: Theologian, Christian, Man for His Times: A Biography*, rev. ed. (Minneapolis: Fortress, 2000) 997n155.

24. Mendelson added, "And it seems hard to imagine how Auden could have encountered Bonhoeffer even if he had been in New York at the time. Auden didn't meet Reinhold Niebuhr until 1940 and, as far as I know, had met no one in theological circles until he met the Niebuhrs" (correspondence with the author, August 10, 2014).

25. Edel, *Writing Lives*, 13.

left-right divides. Some conservatives, including contributors to *Christianity Today* and *First Things*, admired the account for its treatment of the beauty of a Christ-formed celibate same-sex partnership. Some liberals and many members of the guild, including a few who had told me in interviews that they'd always considered Bonhoeffer to be gay, wrote criticisms in blogs, social media posts, or letters to the editor. These protestations seemed to be written out of concern for the Bonhoeffer brand.

"None of us knows whether it was more than a close friendship between Bonhoeffer and the man who became the executor of his literary estate," Barnett writes in her letter to the *New York Times*, objecting to Randall Balmer's review of *Strange Glory*. "I wish that Professor Marsh in what is in many ways a fine book had acknowledged the speculative nature of his conclusions on this point."[26] I had no need to speculate, because the evidence convinced me that the relationship was never consummated sexually. I'm still waiting for Barnett to show me the passage in the first part of *Strange Glory* where I describe "an active homosexual relationship between the two men."

In a letter to her friend Sara Hennell, the novelist George Eliot writes that we must have mercy on critics who are obliged to make a figure in printed pages:

> They must by all means say striking things. Either we should not read printed criticisms at all . . . or we should read them with the constant remembrance that they are a fugitive kind of work which, in the present stage of human nature, can rarely engage a very high grade of conscience or ability. The fate of a book, which is not entirely ephemeral, is never decided by journalists or reviewers of any but an exceptional kind.[27]

---

26. Victoria J. Barnett, "Letters: 'Bonhoeffer, Bethge and Hitler,'" *New York Times*, August 22, 2014, https://www.nytimes.com/2014/08/24/books/review/letters-a-troublesome-inheritance.html; and Balmer, "Between God and the Führer," *New York Times*, August 8, 2014, https://www.nytimes.com/2014/08/10/books/review/strange-glory-a-life-of-dietrich-bonhoeffer-by-charles-marsh.html.

27. Eliot held biographical writing in suspicion while modeling a narrative

Eliot's letter joins a body of commentary around the question of whether authors should respond to their critics, or even read them. But even the most reticent would agree that there are times when maintaining a "dignified silence feels like a moral evasion."[28] Such was the case for me with a review by a German Lutheran pastor and church administrator from the Rhineland named Ferdinand Schlingensiepen.

His criticisms first surfaced in emails to me and then in public lectures, and eventually in published form—in the German-language International Bonhoeffer Society *Rundbrief*, in a German Bonhoeffer Society circular, and in two different English-language online journals (in two different versions).[29] His emails to me alone run upward of a hundred pages.

It has been my practice to resist responding to critics whose reviews seemed the result of personal animus. But when the International Bonhoeffer Society convened its 2016 International Congress in Basel, Switzerland, and invited Schlingensiepen to give a paper and then proceeded to publish the lecture, without inviting a response from me, I realized I would need to mount a detailed rebuttal.

Of course, my desire to do so stems in part from *amour propre*, but I also believe that the substantive differences between the approaches of two noted Bonhoeffer scholars deserve to be clarified.

---

style and moral focus that would influence a new generation of biographers. In *Middlemarch*, Dorothea's "hidden, luminous life commemorates those whose 'unhistoric or obscure acts' have had an 'incalculably diffusive' influence: the number who lived faithfully a hidden life and rest in unvisited tombs'" (Eliot cited in Lee, *Biography*, 68).

28. Lee, *Biography*, 98.

29. See Schlingensiepen, "Making Assumptions about Dietrich." Throughout this book, I refer to the English language critiques as "the review."

WHY, AND WHY NOW?

While, of course, I want to defend against spurious criticisms, and also admit mistakes where I've made them, I also want this short book to highlight the broader implications of this exchange with Schlingensiepen. These implications are at least threefold, for the Bonhoeffer guild as well as the enterprise of theological biography.

The first implication is the question of reliance on canonical accounts of a biographical subject. To what degree ought biographers be bound to what the field considers authoritative texts, such as Bethge's biography? Or what ability—and freedom—should they feel to challenge, expand, and alter the canon of their subject based on new materials or simply a new perspective or methodology?

The second major difference is regarding openness to ambiguity in a life, especially in the lives of one's heroes. *Strange Glory* presents Bonhoeffer replete with compromises and complexities, secrets and mystery. Biographers ought not fear rendering their subjects more human but, indeed, should aim to write accounts that resound with those tensions that give life its vitality.

Finally, this dispute highlights the particular insights available to theological biography, a mode of biography and storytelling that attends to the interactions between a subject's theology (or the predominant theology or worldview of the subject's culture) and the plot and relationships in the subject's life—which is to say, it's a narrative mode that may enliven not only the biographical subject but also doctrine itself (*enliven* here in the near-literal sense—showing doctrine as it appears when flared by a human life).

Strange Glory was published in April 2014; the German translation, *Dietrich Bonhoeffer: Der verklärte Fremde. Eine Biografie*, was published in March 2015 by Gütersloher Verlagshaus. At first, I followed the lead of my editor and writer friends who cautioned me against the aggrieved author clapback. Then a month in the summer of 2021 opened up unexpectedly—I completed a book manuscript on deadline (which is to say, my most recently negotiated deadline) and I'd recovered from COVID-19, but my professional calendar had not. It seemed like a good time to write a response.

In Schlingensiepen's view, Bethge's 1969 book is the guild's canonical scripture by which all biographical accounts of Bonhoeffer must be governed. I can say with confidence that Bethge would not have made any such pontifical claim over his own work. The appeal to an interpretive authority instead serves Schlingensiepen's purpose of imposing tempers and dispositions, rules and regulations, in writing Bonhoeffer's life. That his own effort resembles more a compendium of facts than "the presence of an approachable life" exemplifies the stultifying effect of this canonical fetish. It's biography written out of obligation. Barnett's plan to deepen our understanding of Bonhoeffer's "personality" by writing a biographical account based on "external church influences" further illustrates the limitations of this constraining mandate.

Schlingensiepen brings this straitjacket of dogma to bear on his criticism of *Strange Glory*, but he is only half right about my use of Bethge's biography. I did read the 1970 abridged English-language edition several times during my doctoral studies and early teaching years, along with sections from the 1,128-page Christian Kaiser Verglag edition, *Dietrich Bonhoeffer: A Biographie. Theologe, Christ, Zeitgenosse*. And when Fortress Press published the unabridged English-language edition in 2000, I worked through the 1,048-page biography with ruminative devotion.

But Schlingensiepen is correct that I did not use it as a road map or appropriate its narrative structure. I tried to draw sparingly from its unparalleled riches, as I sought to create a portrait inspired by new archival discoveries, interviews, and primary documents, as well as the completed sixteen-volume *Dietrich Bonhoeffer Works*. I never thought of my approach as a repudiation of Bethge's magisterial work but as a tribute to its completeness.

Schlingensiepen's biography was published in 2006 in a wave of books commemorating the hundredth anniversary of Bonhoeffer's birth; the year before had marked the seventieth anniversary of his death in 1945. It was a busy time for Bonhoeffer scholars.

His book was reviewed in most major German newspapers: *Frankfurter Allgemeine Zeitung (FAZ) Die Zeit, Süddeutsche Zeitung, Neue Zürcher Zeitung (NZZ) Die Welt,* as well as on national public radio. Overall, it was positively received, lauded as a well-researched and evenhanded portrayal. Sometimes it was discussed in tandem with Sabine Dramm's 2005 book, *V-Mann Gottes und der Abwehr? Dietrich Bonhoeffer und der Widerstand,* translated as *Dietrich Bonhoeffer and the Resistance* in 2009.

Writing in the *Frankfurter Allgemeine Zeitung,* Peter Steinbach compliments Schlingensiepen's overall effort but recommends Dramm's as the superior volume because of her deft handling of Bonhoeffer's "inner contradictions" and complex involvements in the German resistance. Steinbach writes, "Schlingensiepen does not succeed like Sabine Dramm in showing the tensions and contradictions of a man who every day faced the agonizing decisions of dissident life in a dictatorial system, and who at the same time moved through that system as a conspirator—as a man whose duplicity required him to live in twilight."[30]

Schlingensiepen began conveying his thoughts to me in emails shortly after my book was published. His first notes struck a collegial tone. He writes in an email on May 30, 2014:

> I am reading your book with great interest, learning a lot. Thank you for letting me have it. I could now break out in the praise your book deserves. But right now I have another motive for writing to you.
>
> From time to time I come across a minor fault; and as there will be a German edition no doubt, I think you should know about it.

---

30. Peter Steinbach, "Seelsorger des Widerstands," *Frankfurter Allgemeine Zeitung,* November 12, 2005, https://www.faz.net/aktuell/feuilleton/politik/seelsorger-des-widerstands-1282935.html. "Schlingensiepen gelingt es nicht wie Sabine Dramm, die Widersprüche eines Menschen zu zeichnen, der sich in einem diktatorischen System tagtäglich entscheiden mußte, der zunächst keine Kompromisse einging, der sich dann auf eine Mitarbeit im Zentrum der Macht einließ. Das tat er, um das Regime zu überwinden. Und zugleich rückte er dennoch in das System hinein, lebte im Zwielicht. Schließlich wollte er die Niederlage, weil er Deutschland liebte."

What do you suggest: Should I make a list and mail it to you? You could then decide if you will alter your text a little bit. (It could of course be that you think that I am wrong.)

I find that between first and second editions one has always to do a bit of "mending." If you want to see my list of questions, please let me have your mail address.

The next letter, sent via email on August 12, 2014, strikes a different chord. He says that after reading *Strange Glory* twice "I can only say that your book has disturbed me." And he adds, "Your picture of Bonhoeffer is so far away from mine that I feel I have to write a review pointing out our differences."

The collegial promise of a list of edits to include in the second edition had given way to a campaign to discredit the book and its author.

In what follows, I've organized Schlingensiepen's criticisms in five categories, and I respond to each in kind. I am not entirely sure which of Schlingensiepen's numerous drafts—sent to me by Schlingensiepen himself and members of the International Bonhoeffer Society—were also presented as lectures at scholarly conferences or circulated through the society. I will base my responses on the three versions in my possession: (1) "Making Assumptions About Dietrich: How Bonhoeffer was Made Fit for America," (2) "American Biographies Co-opt Bonhoeffer: Looking at Charles Marsh's *A Life of Dietrich Bonhoeffer* with a Brief Glance at the Contrasting Book by Eric Metaxas" (the review coauthored with Heiner Süselbeck, a colleague of Schlingensiepen in the Evangelische Kirche im Rheinland) and (3) a longer draft of the same piece sent to me by the author.[31]

---

31. See Schlingensiepen, "Making Assumptions about Dietrich"; Ferdinand Schlingensiepen and Heiner Süselbeck, "American Biographies Co-opt Bonhoeffer: Looking at Charles Marsh's A Life of Dietrich Bonhoeffer with a Brief Glance at the Contrasting Book by Eric Metaxas," the International Dietrich Bonhoeffer Group *Rundbrief*, 2014.

I. Mea Culpa: Factual and Geographical Errors

In the fall of 2015, Schlingensiepen conveyed his thoughts to me via numerous emails and rough drafts of his review essay that would eventually become the published essays. I am grateful to him for pointing out a number of factual errors in the first printing.

For example, I was off on the location of Bayreuth by a hundred kilometers. Friedrichsbrunn is a hunting lodge, not a forester's lodge. Julius Rieger is at one point accidentally named Justin Rieger. The ecumenical conference took place in Chamby, not Chambry. Dachau lies to the northwest of Munich, not to the northeast. And the Eisenach River does not flow at the foot of the Wartburg Castle in the village named Eisenach.

Other minor errors that escaped my attention: I incorrectly named a Berlin department store and attributed the reproduction of a woodcut on a postcard to the wrong person. I should have said that in 1933 there were six thousand clergy—not members—in the Confessing Church. Likewise, a footnote calling Bethel an extension of the T4 euthanasia program is a mistake that I should have caught at the time. In fact, I noted elsewhere that several preachers, including Ernst Wilm, spoke courageously against euthanasia and were punished for their actions by being sent to the Dachau concentration camp. On the website of the Project on Lived Theology, you will find a recording of a presentation by Leroy Walters, the former Joseph P. Kennedy Sr. Professor of Christian Ethics at the Kennedy Institute of Ethics at Georgetown University, on the T4 program and killing centers developed in 1939 by Nazi doctors.[32] In my seminar on theology in the Third Reich, Walters discussed his research on bioethics under national socialism, specifically with regard to how three of Bonhoeffer's writings—a letter, a sermon, and the discussion of "life unworthy of life" in his never-completed *Ethics*—gave distinct theological form to Paul Gerhard Braune's rejection of the regime's euthanasia initiative. In the remarkable essay on which the presentation was based, "Dietrich Bonhoeffer

32. Walters, "Dietrich Bonhoeffer Confronts Nazi Eugenics and Euthanasia," The Project on Lived Theology, February 28, 2012, https://www.livedtheology.org/resources/dietrich-bonhoeffer-confronts-nazi-eugenics-and-euthanasia/

Confronts Nazi Eugenics and Euthanasia," Walters says, "Through their courage and perseverance Braune and von Bodelschwingh were able to protect their patients in Bethel and Lobetal, but they could not bring a halt to the relentless T4 killing program. One can only wish, with the benefit of hindsight, that Braune, in solidarity with the entire Inner Mission organization—and indeed all the leaders of the Protestant and Catholic churches—had gone public with the information that they had in the summer of 1940."[33]

Indeed, Bonhoeffer's contributions to the Bethel Declaration and sharp disagreement with Barth over the theological meaning of the Aryan Clause strikes me as an episode in the *Kirchenkampf* still largely unexamined in Anglo-American circles. Moreover, these implications bear profoundly on the current political situation in the United States. I would point to the chapter titled "Theological Storm Troopers on the March," in which I portray the twenty-seven-year-old Bonhoeffer insisting that the German Church's support of the Aryan Clause signaled its apostasy. Barth thought not and advised a more cautious path: dissident Christians should not renounce the German Evangelical Church but remain in the church *in statu confessionis*. More direct opposition to the church "should await something more doctrinally decisive than the Aryan Clause," which Barth did not find a sufficient reason to abandon "the sinking ship."[34]

---

33. See also Ernst Klee, *Euthanasie im NS-Staat: Die Vernichtung lebensunweren Lebens* (Frankfurt: S. Fischer Verlag, 1983) 338–39. However, there is perhaps an ambiguity in this counterfactual wish. Institutional leaders like Braune and von Bodelschwingh would have risked being sent to concentration camps or executed had they gone public, and it is possible that the patients housed in Bethel and Lobetal would have been killed in retaliation for their leaders' "opposition to what the regime considered to be important state programs" (Klee, *Euthanasie*). In a 1986 interview with Barnett, Berta Braune, Paul Braune's wife, distinguished the roles of the preacher or prophet, on the one hand, and facility director, on the other. She argued that the administrator's top priority was to protect the people entrusted to his or her care. Several ministers, including Wilm, preached publicly against the euthanasia program and were sent to the Dachau concentration camp as punishment. See Barnett, *For the Soul of the People: Protestant Protest against Hitler* (New York: Oxford University Press, 1992) 116, 322n61, 179.

34. Marsh, *Strange Glory*, 185.

"I know there are many who await your opinion," Bonhoeffer writes to Barth in a letter dated September 9, 1933, "and I also know that most think you will counsel us to wait until we are thrown out. However, some of us have already been thrown out, namely, the Jewish Christians, and the same will soon happen to the others." The paragraph, he still contends, had separated "the Prussian church from Christianity" and "committed blasphemy against the Holy Spirit, which cannot be forgiven in either this world or the next."[35]

Historical errors, no matter the scope, are a problem and merit correction. I follow a distinguished lineage of biographers and scholars in offering a heartfelt mea culpa.

However, the claim that these errata evince "laissez faire treatment of sources" is unjustified. In the company I keep, getting the name of a department store wrong is not generally considered "particularly grotesque." My identification of the Bonhoeffer's country house in the eastern Harz mountains—which I visited in the spring of 2011, retracing Bonhoeffer's steps in this region he dearly loved—as a forester's lodge is a garden variety mistake easily corrected in a new printing. To conclude that these mistakes call for "nothing short of a complete rewriting" is to make one's bed with internet trolls. It's the kind of indignation and rage that, to quote James Parker's amusing essay on the subject, "seems to predate you somehow."[36]

Consider further his contretemps with my view of the Bonhoeffer family's religious observance. "[Karl Bonhoeffer] accepted his wife's instruction of the children only in measured doses, and only so long as it served a useful purpose," I write. I further observe that he did not attend church on Sundays but left this to his wife and children.[37] Initially, Schlingensiepen allows that this is a small

35. This paragraph is reprinted with permission from Marsh, *Strange Glory*, 186.

36. James Parker and Zoe Heller, "Should Writers Respond to Their Critics?" *New York Times*, December 16, 2014, https://www.nytimes.com/2014/12/21/books/review/should-writers-respond-to-their-critics.html.

37. Schlingensiepen, "Making Assumptions about Dietrich"; Marsh, *Strange Glory*, 8.

thing. But he's got a bee in his bonnet and can't stop swatting: "We consider that it attributes to Bonhoeffer the kind of socialization in the church that the future pastor did not have."

Not only is Schlingensiepen wrong to say that Paula Bonhoeffer did not go to church—all the children were baptized and confirmed—his charge that I attribute to Bonhoeffer "a socialization in the church" through the guidance of his mother and siblings is a complete misreading. Nowhere in the book do I propose that the young Dietrich was a diligent churchgoer or that his spiritual upbringing was in any significant part shaped by regularly attending church service at an early age. In fact, I say the opposite, pointing to the journal entries from his mass-crawling Roman holiday during Holy Week of 1924—each day marked by another "magnifico!"—which reveal the extent of his boredom with north German Lutheranism.

Schlingensiepen's criticism is an ungenerous and seemingly willful misreading of the text with accusations either blown entirely out of proportion or amounting to outright falsehoods, such as his remark that my "manuscript needed . . . substantial corrections . . . before being published in Germany" or that the "content of Marsh's biography will have to change in the German version." This is patently false.[38]

Although I make no claim to infallibility (and am grateful for the opportunity to correct errors) it is mind-boggling that someone who has publicly accused another—to pick the most charitable interpretation—of fatal omissions is guilty of the same in a document whose sole purpose is to justify those charges.[39]

---

38. On April 4, 2018, I wrote to my German editor: "Do you have any recollection of the matters mentioned below—the 'substantial corrections'—on which FS says he consulted with you?" My editor replied: "There is only one small list from January 2, 2015. On half a page Clifford Green noted some errors regarding some quotations from *Barcelona, Berlin, New York*, but nothing important. Victoria Barnett sent nothing. So—much ado about nothing."

39. Counter to Schlingensiepen's claim, Julius Rieger was *Studieninspektor* at the Naumburger Predigerseminar in 1927 before he became a priest at St George's German Lutheran Church in East London. Fanø is an island in the Danish North Sea, not, as Schlingensiepen claims, the Baltic Sea. To say Theodor Fontane *visited* the Harz Mountains, as Schlingensiepen eagerly suggests

Although most of these omissions and inaccuracies are as minor as my own—I've put a few of them in a footnote—Schlingensiepen's claim that Bonhoeffer did not enter the political resistance out of his vocation as a pastor-theologian in the Confessing Church but as brother-in-law of Hans von Dohnanyi deserves critical attention.[40] Is Schlingensiepen suggesting that Bonhoeffer's participation in the conspiracy was motivated by familial loyalty alone? It is true, as Sabine Dramm notes, that Bonhoeffer did not write a systematic theology of resistance: "Bonhoeffer was not the theologian of the resistance." But as an ordained pastor and "theologian in the resistance," every aspect of his life, and most decisively his opposition to Hitler, counted among the costs of discipleship.[41] Since Schlingensiepen claims that I have fallen short of rigorous professional standards, I am tempted to wonder whether the formula by which he arrived at such conclusions is a standard of proof he would have accepted from his graduate and undergraduate students. Even if the answer is yes, I am certain that no one—besides the inhabitants of that little island called the International Bonhoeffer Society—would reasonably consider what he has presented here as proof that my research is flawed.

---

in an apparent correction, is to imply, at least in the English language, that he merely went there on a brief trip, whereas on four occasions during the summer, Fontane lived in the opulent Hotel Zehnpfund. Schlingensiepen says that I was wrong to have the emperor's children play in the Tiergarten. "Besides," he adds, "they were not the emperor's children, they were his grand-children." Sabine Leibholz-Bonhoeffer, Dietrich's twin sister, says otherwise. In her family memoir, she writes: "My parents first home in Berlin was near the Tiergarten, with windows looking out on the Bellevue Park. Our governess, a monarchist in heart and soul, took a great interest in the Kaiser's children, who played there." Might I be forgiven for assuming Bellevue Park counts as part of the Tiergarten and for favoring the more widely known Tiergarten to the specific Bellevue Park, to allow an English-speaking reader a better sense of location for this scene?

40. This claim is asserted without explanation in Schlingensiepen and Süselbeck, "American Biographies Co-opt Bonhoeffer."

41. Dramm, *Dietrich Bonhoeffer and the Resistance*, trans. Margaret Kohl (Minneapolis: Fortress, 2009) 239.

II. Sins of omission

Schlingensiepen further claims that material not covered in my biography, or covered insufficiently, reveals major defects in the book. Most of these criticisms pertain to Lutheran ecclesial history and polity and serve as a stage on which he flatters himself with lengthy recitations on German church minutiae of the sort found in his biography.

Consider the following.

Schlingensiepen is dismayed that I skip over two articles Bonhoeffer wrote after returning to Berlin from England in 1935.[42]

> Why doesn't Marsh tell his readers that Hitler created a Ministry of Church in 1935 under the direction of Hans [sic] Kerrl, whom he instructed to end the *Kirchenstreit*? Subsequently, Kerrl wanted to coerce the Confessing Church into forming a common committee with the heretic "German Christians" (*die deutsche Christen*) and their leader Wilhelm Zoellner. Why this was no longer an option after the synod of Dahlem is something Bonhoeffer himself describes clearly in his papers on *Die Bekennende Kirche und die Ökumene* and in his essay on *Kirchengemeinschaft*. No reader of a biography on Bonhoeffer can truly understand the "arch-Dahlemite" Bonhoeffer without having been properly informed on the synod of Dahlem. Otherwise, the difference between "functioning" and "dysfunctional" churches and the reason why "functioning" churches, in the eyes of Bonhoeffer, were false, heretic compromises remains unaccounted for. The fact that West German churches of the old-Prussian Union had become less subservient through the influence of the reformists should be of interest even to American readers.

I'm not sure whether this is an example of a rhetorical or tautological question. Schlingensiepen does a fine job demonstrating reasons why I chose not to warble over Kerrl, in any case.

He's not finished:

42. Bonhoeffer wrote more than two articles during this period; Schlingensiepen didn't specify which two.

"The names of Oberheid and Jaeger are missing."

"The name Zoellner is also missing from Marsh's text."

"Kerrl is mentioned once, only in a context outside of the timeframe when he was trying to unify the disparate Protestant church under the leadership of the committees."

"Gertrud Staewen gets mentioned . . . but other courageous women like Katharina Staritz or men like Propst Grueber do not appear."[43]

43. Ironically, Staritz does not appear in Schlingensiepen's book, but I wish I had been able to include her remarkable story. Katharina Helene Charlotte Staritz was a Protestant theologian from Bonhoeffer's birth town of Breslau who studied Protestant theology in Marburg and was one of the first women with a doctorate in theology or to serve as an active pastor in the Protestant church. In 1938, she took over the management of the Kirchliche Hilfsstelle für evangelische Nichtarier (Church Aid Centre for Protestant Non-Aryans) and was officially responsible for the church care of Jews and their relatives. This meant that together with Pastor Heinrich Grüber, she organized accommodation, procured false passports, and helped Jews and Christians with Jewish parents or grandparents emigrate. This became nearly impossible after 1939 and required Katharina and her sister, Charlotte, to work underground to do everything they could to save Jewish citizens. Through these efforts, she saved more than one hundred people from the Nazi terror, unlike many of her pastor colleagues. In September 1941, she wrote an open letter to the pastors in Breslau, clearly opposing the state's decree that Jews have to wear the Star of David: "It is the Christian duty of the congregations not to exclude them [Jewish Christians] from church services, for example because of the marking. They have the same right of residence in the church as the other members of the congregation and are in particular need of comfort from God's word. The congregations are in danger of being misled by elements that are not Christian, that may jeopardize the Christian honor of the Church by un-Christian behavior. They are in need of pastoral care, for example by referring to Luke 10, 25–37, Matthew 25, 40." The Silesian church leadership suspended her from her duties at the aid station, and then she was taken into "protective custody," transferred to a police prison in Kassel in March 1942, sent to the work education camp at Breitenau in 1942, and then imprisoned with the political prisoners at the Ravensbrück concentration camp. Through the efforts of her sister and Paul Graf Yorck von Wartenburg, she received a "probationary" release. Following the war, she received a sermon and pastoral care assignment at St. Katharinen-Gemeinde—the first pastoral position for a woman in Hesse— though she still had to bear the title vicar. Her poems and letters written during her imprisonment were published posthumously under the title *Des großen Lichtes Widerschein*. See Katharina von Kellenbach, "Dialogue in Times of War: Christian Women's Rescue of Jews in Hitler's Germany," in *Women and*

Also missing: "a lawyer by the name of Dr. Friedrich Werner."

Without these persons and institutions, Schlingensiepen says he "could not gain a sense of Bonhoeffer's life and his positioning during this period in his life."

And once again but with emphasis: "The truly unsettling aspect of Marsh's book is that he didn't take the trouble to understand the organizational structure of the *Deutsche Evangelische Kirche* and its 28 *Landeskirchen*." Schlingensiepen's tendentious account goes as follows: Bonhoeffer's prescience; his early, lacerating critique of the führer; his concern for civil liberties; his global, ecumenical sensibilities; his call for concrete political protest; and his subversive teaching on the Sermon on the Mount were, in Schlingensiepen's view, convictions widely held by Confessing Church pastors. He writes that "hundreds were imprisoned long before Bonhoeffer, some of them for a short time, others for longer. The majority of them are not mentioned by Marsh." That may be true, but throughout his biography, Schlingensiepen's priorities lie more with the reputation of the Confessing Church than in catching the "light-beams" (in Thomas Carlyle's apt summation of written lives) that make up the subject's character. [44] In fact, Schlingensiepen's entire project of defending the Confessing Church requires him to denigrate Bonhoeffer as entirely average. The narrative challenge of including hundreds of pastors in the supporting cast of a written life is daunting. What do you do with them all?

Interreligious Dialogue, ed. Catherine Cornille and Jillian Maxey (Eugene, OR: Wipf & Stock, 2013) 76–87; Wolfgang Gerlach, *And the Witnesses Were Silent: The Confessing Church and the Persecution of the Jews*, ed. and trans. Victoria J. Barnett (Lincoln, NE: University of Nebraska Press, 2000) 169–73.

44. Carlyle, *Oliver Cromwell's Letters and Speeches with Elucidations* (Boston, MA: Standard, 1899) 3:288. Among Schlingensiepen's aggrieved enumerations is his dismay of my use of the word *coterie* in reference to Bonhoeffer's allies at Dahlem, which Schlingensiepen considers "the most important synod of the Confessing Church." He says that Bonhoeffer and Bethge would have turned in their graves if they had seen my sentence—how dare I "degrade" the reputation of the church dissidents by calling it a "coterie"? He'd looked up the word in a dictionary to confirm his suspicions that I'd actually called the Dahlemites "a scheming group of people." This is not scholarly discussion; it is the sound of a captious pedant.

The pedantry of his assertations—"*X* gets mentioned only once or twice"; "there is no mention of"; "what Marsh ought to have written"; "Marsh didn't really understand"—obscures the more important point at hand. Selectivity is biography's principal virtue—and necessity.

But before we pulp the inventory, let me ask a question. Is this tyrannical mastery of Lutheran ecclesial minutiae from 1933 to 1945 really what we're after when we settle into the life of Bonhoeffer?

I choose not to describe in detail the different stages of the Protestant church's *Gleichschaltung* for the very reason Schlingensiepen allows in his conclusion: "The fate of the 'German Protestant Church' in Hitler's Germany will interest very few people in Germany today. Outside of Germany the complexities will be comprehensible only to specialists." Instead, I supplied information about the German Evangelical Church in tolerable doses and in service to character.[45]

More germane to the written life at hand: by 1939 Bonhoeffer was done with good German churchmen. For most American nonspecialists, the Confessing Church is assumed to be an anti-Nazi theological movement led by dissident churchmen such as Bonhoeffer, Karl Barth, and Martin Niemöller. But the Confessing Church's opposition to state control of the churches did not preclude collaboration with, or indifference toward, the regime. As early as 1933, Bonhoeffer had already grasped the limitations of church dissent. Neither the Declaration of Barmen nor Bethel, to take two examples, denounced the Hitler regime or directly contested, in word or application, the Nazi persecution of the Jewish people.

This commitment to character applies as well to the amount of attention I give Bonhoeffer's church contacts abroad, which Schlingensiepen thinks is insufficient. He expects of my

---

45. *Gleichschaltung*, as defined by the Wiener Holocaust Center, is "the process of the Nazi Party taking control over all aspects of Germany. It is otherwise known as coordination or Nazification" ("How Did the Nazi Consolidate Their Power?," Wiener Holocaust Center, https://www.theholocaustexplained.org/the-nazi-rise-to-power/how-did-the-nazi-gain-power/gleichschaltung/).

biography nothing less than the ecumenical life launderings that cycle through his treatise. "Ignoring the close cooperation between Anglican Bishop Bell and Bonhoeffer in their fight for the Confessing Church during Bonhoeffer's time in London," Schlingensiepen says, renders my account of the Fanø conference "completely useless" (*völlig unbrauchtbar*).

Nevertheless, George Bell, the Bishop of Chichester and president of Life and Work at the ecumenical council in Geneva, who issued a pastoral letter on behalf of the Confessing Front, as the Confessing Church was called in these months before its first major synod, appears as "Bell" fifty-nine times in *Strange Glory*, always in reference to the Kirchenkampf. Yet—and please bear with me on this point—despite his fallacious claim that I marginalized Bishop Bell in my account, Bonhoeffer as a person goes largely missing in Schlingensiepen.

Fanø is one of my favorite episodes related to Bonhoeffer's subversive devotion to the Sermon on the Mount. For the cover of my first book—a study of Bonhoeffer's early philosophical theology—I was pleased when Gütersloher Verlagshaus permitted me to use a photo of Bonhoeffer reposed on the dunes near Fanø with his students Inge Karding, Lotte Kühn, O. Dudzus, and "an unknown Swede," even though thinking biographically about Bonhoeffer was not my concern in 1994.

I knew little about his life beyond the purview of his academic involvements. In *Strange Glory*, I chose to highlight Bonhoeffer's bold intonations of peace, to build the narrative around scenes involving the group of students that would come to be known as the "Deutsches Fanø."

That Fanø was a defining moment in Bonhoeffer's journey to nonviolence is lost amid Schlingensiepen's obsessive wish to put the German church participants in the best possible light. He gives us such tendentious reports as this: "It looked for a while as though [Bonhoeffer] were going to cancel his participation in Fanø, especially when the Confessing Church representatives decided not to go *because of the political situation in Germany;* but they, like the two bishops, were convinced that Bonhoeffer must be there." Schlingensiepen would have us believe that the Confessing Church representatives were not able to attend the conference because of inescapable political constraints, when in fact they could have been on the next ferry to Copenhagen without a hitch. Just like Bonhoeffer and his students.

Another odd feature of Schlingensiepen's account of Fanø is the casual way he refers to the Nazi churchman Theodor Heckel as "Bonhoeffer's opponent" as if the two were competing in a debate tournament. And he fails to note Heckel's role as one of Hitler's most trustworthy apparatchiks. His dismissal of my unflattering portrayal of Heckel and the other German nationalists sent to Denmark to silence dissident voices reads more like a scold than a historiographic intervention.

If one recalls Schlingensiepen's misleading aside in his biography that "In Fanø . . . Bonhoeffer encountered more agreement than criticism," it is clear, I think, that his fire and fury serve the double purpose of deflecting attention from some of his dubious claims.[46]

Bonhoeffer's remarks in Denmark marked him one of Germany's most conspicuous Christian dissidents. It was here that he delivered his first major address on Christ and peace and as a result

---

46. Schlingensiepen, *Dietrich Bonhoeffer 1906–1945: Martyr, Thinker, Man of Resistance*, trans. Isabel Best (London: T. & T. Clark, 2010) 171–72.

positioned himself at the front of a radical theological movement that broke from the tradition of German martial Protestantism. It is my view that Fanø shows an emergent Bonhoeffer who is more subversive than the great majority of the Confessing Church—a point that Schlingensiepen does not wish to grant (and that most readers of his biography seem to miss). This tradition of martial Protestantism was Bonhoeffer's birthright as a member of the German Protestant Church, and until his turn to a peace ethic during the American year, it's a tradition he had fully embraced.

In his first doctoral dissertation *Sanctorum Communio*, completed in 1927, Bonhoeffer writes of a will of God that is aligned with the will of people. This casual Christian nationalism made it easy for him to say: "Where a people, submitting in conscience to God's will, goes to war in order to fulfill its historical purpose and mission in the world—though entering fully into the ambiguity of human sinful action—it knows it has been called upon by God, that history is to be made; here war is no longer murder."[47] Killing the enemy, he says, can even be called an act of love under these conditions.

Fast forward to 1934 and the modest guest room on the west coast of Denmark, with the windows open to the brisk North Sea air (not the Baltic) where Bonhoeffer writes "The Church and the Peoples of the World" based on a verse in Psalm 85. He delivered the speech on August 28, 1934. He speaks of a day when the church would resolve to become an agent of the promised peace rather than another force of violence. He speaks of communities of discipleship formed by the teachings of Jesus, obedient without reserve to his commandments. He speaks of the urgency of Christians beginning again with the affirmation that the church of Jesus Christ exists at one and the same time in all peoples, beyond all national boundaries, political, social, or racial:

> All who confess Jesus Christ as Lord, are quite necessarily, and ontologically, members of and citizens in the

47. Bonhoeffer, *DBWE: Sanctorum Communio: A Theological Study of the Sociology of the Church*, ed. Clifford J. Green (Minneapolis: Fortress, 1998) 1:119.

global, ecumenical church; brothers [and sisters] bound
together . . . more inseparably than people who share the
ties of history, kin, class, and language . . . . The hour is
late. . . . The world is choked with weapons, and dreadful
is the mistrust peering from all men's eyes. What are we
waiting for? Peace must be dared. . . . Peace is the great
venture.[48]

Christ is peace.

Back in Berlin, a group of young Christians gravitated to
Bonhoeffer, "seriously considering the possibility of starting a
small Christian community, some kind of settlement inspired by
the Sermon on the Mount." Out of a church aligned closely with
state power, the Bonhoeffer circle "would . . . make a definite stand
for peace by conscientious objection" and carry a subversive new
message forward, circulating and discussing the speeches and ad-
dresses of that summer.[49]

Schlingensiepen would find this address unremarkable. He
writes, "Such *amiable* formulations meet with success at most
conferences; the one in Fanø was no exception."[50] Time and again,
Schlingensiepen dampens the fire of Bonhoeffer's convictions out
of a pernicious desire to fit him into the mold of the "good German
churchman." The result is the flattening of character and an exag-
geration of the Confessing Church's protest against Hitler.

In recent years, it has become the consensus of the International Bonhoeffer Society to commend Schlingensiepen's biography as the one to read if you're not ready for Bethge's 1,000-page
life. In a recent article in *Patheos* entitled "The Integrity of Dietrich
Bonhoeffer: Please, Read Anything But Metaxas!," a Lutheran pastor toes the party line in calling *Martyr, Thinker, Man of Resistance*
the "best and most faithful of the recent biographies." He feels
this strongly because Hermann Schlingensiepen, the biographer's

48. Bonhoeffer quoted in Marsh, *Strange Glory*, 213.

49. Bonhoeffer quoted in Marsh, *Strange Glory*, 215.

50. Schlingensiepen, *Dietrich Bonhoeffer 1906–1945*, 170. For more on
Bonhoeffer's pacifist ideas see Clifford J. Green, "Pacifism and Tyrannicide:
Bonhoeffer's Christian Peace Ethic," *Studies in Christian Ethics* 18 (2005)
31–47.

father, "served as a principal of one of the seminaries of the confessing church, and Ferdinand Schlingensiepen, the principal's
son, was a close friend of Eberhard Bethge, best friend of Bonhoeffer[,] and [an] editor of his collected works in German . . . as well
as one of the founding members of the International Bonhoeffer
Society." The author of the *Patheos* article said he'd read *Strange
Glory* over the Christmas holidays and enjoyed it but that he also
knew "enough of the conversation happening in the International
Bonhoeffer Society around it to not accept it as a wholesale and
helpful reading of Bonhoeffer's life."[51]

Capable theological minds have passed blithely over passages
in Schlingensiepen's book that consistently understate or ignore
the Confessing Church's failure to speak out boldly against Hitler and to act concretely on behalf of the Jewish people; which is
to say, they ignore its complicity in the Holocaust. In Bonhoeffer
studies and modern Protestant thought more broadly, you hear the
Declaration of Barmen and the Confessing Church routinely cited
as exemplars of "radical" Christian conviction. Barmen raised "its
voice against Hitler's in post-Weimar Republican Germany," a
Presbyterian writer minister writes.[52]

As theological speech, the 1934 Barmen Declaration registers
a fierce protest against idolatry, affirming that the lordship of Jesus
Christ brings judgment upon all the ways the righteous God becomes tethered to ideology and profaned. "We reject the false doctrine, as though the Church in human arrogance could place the
Word and work of the Lord in the service of any arbitrarily chosen
desires, purposes, and plans."[53] This passage—and the entire theo-

51. Clint Schnekloth, "The Integrity of Dietrich Bonhoeffer: Please,
Read Anything but Metaxas!," *Patheos*, June 22, 2020, https://www.
patheos.com/blogs/clintschnekloth/2020/06/the-integrity-of-dietrich
-bonhoeffer-april-9th-70-years-after-his-death/.

52. St. Andrews Presbyterian Church, "Do You Know What a Confession
Is? . . . as a Presbyterian (PCUSA) You Should," *Facebook*, January 11, 2017,
https://www.facebook.com/saintandrewspc/posts/604441769755116/.

53. "The Theological Declaration of Barmen," in *The Constitution of the
Presbyterian Church (U.S.A.): Part I, Book of Confessions* (Louisville: Office of
General Assembly of the Presbyterian Church [USA] 2016) 284.

logical declaration—belongs among the great creeds of the church. But Barmen did not raise its voice against Hitler.

Schlingensiepen's account reinforces a collective dishonesty about the Confessing Church's relationship to Judaism and shows a blindness to Bonhoeffer's own discontent—if not disgust—with its final capitulation. Contrary to Schlingensiepen, I will state without hesitation that Bonhoeffer's dissident imagination grew out of distinct powers of discernment, suspicion, empathy, and confidence. *Hilaritas*, in other words.

The independent scholar Sabine Dramm, in her superb book *Dietrich Bonhoeffer and the Resistance*, observes the Confessing Church's inaction and Bonhoeffer's existential uncertainties with a sharp unforgiving eye; her book deserves a wider reading audience. The resistance was not a movement one joined but a process.[54] And Bonhoeffer's primary importance in the resistance, according to Dramm, "lies in the ethical foundation for resistance that he offered. . . . The 'internal role' that he played in his resistance circle can most readily be described as 'intellectual pastoral care.'"[55] Schlingensiepen complains that I did not more emphatically and enthusiastically portray Bonhoeffer as a "true Dahlemite." My failure in this department, he continues, "casts doubt on [my] understanding of Bonhoeffer's theology . . . *to the extent that it calls for a complete re-writing.*"

Let the record show that in *Strange Glory* I write the following:

> Only two months after classes began, the Old Prussian Union Council decided that the Confessing Church might call itself a "confessional movement" or "confessional front," but it did not have the legitimate status of a *Kirche* (church). Thus, study with Bonhoeffer became a badge of dissent, and in the eyes of the church authorities it was to mark oneself out as "radical fanatic" and as a disloyal German. Such pastors might sometimes be called "Dahlemites," after the posh Berlin suburb of Dahlem. Moreover, Martin Niemöller's parish, where

54. Dramm, *Dietrich Bonhoeffer and the Resistance*, 19.
55. Dramm, *Dietrich Bonhoeffer and the Resistance*, 7.

a coterie of dissenting ministers had defied the Reich Church, proclaimed the Confessing Church as the one true Lutheran church in Germany.[56]

These are important details. Still, it's hard to imagine an editor or reader who after reading the paragraph would stop, scratch her chin, and write in the margin, "I'll be honest. It was sounding great. But I could've used a little more of 'Zoellner and all the committees.'"

Schlingensiepen's biography reflects a principle of selectivity that favors the image of the good German, a man not unlike so many other courageous pastors in the rank and file of the Confessing Church. A man not unlike his own father.

Schlingensiepen's principle enables him in turn to omit details in his biography that inconvenience the heroic narrative of the good dissident German churchman.

He is correct to point out that no river runs through the village of Eisenach. But his gotcha belies an invidious omission; namely, the very reason I followed Bonhoeffer's journey into Thuringia. As Bonhoeffer traveled with Bethge in March 1938, the by-then familiar sight of Nazi banners draped on homes, buildings, and churches sickened him. As the Wartburg Castle came into view, he could see that the cross that had once framed the entrance was gone, and in its place waved a massive swastika. It was in this hunting lodge, owned by the duke of Saxony, that Luther took refuge in 1521 and translated the New Testament in a feverish ten-week stretch. Four centuries later, Nazi churchmen spoke of their mission to complete the work of Martin Luther.[57]

Although it was Holy Week during their travels, most of Bonhoeffer's countrymen were celebrating Hitler's annexation of Austria. In disgust, Bonhoeffer and Bethge abruptly ended their

---

56. Marsh, *Strange Glory*, 234–35.

57. Wilson Niwagila, "The Church Struggle during the Nazi Period," in *Changing Relations Between Churches in Europe and Africa: The Internationalization of Christianity and Politics in the 20th Century*, ed. Katharina Kunter and Jens Holger Schøjrring (Wiesbaden, Germany: Otto Harrassowitz Verlag, 2008) 47.

journey, diverting to the refuge of the Bonhoeffer country house in Friedrichsbrunn. This story goes unnoticed in both Bethge's and Schlingensiepen's biographies.

The riverless Eisenach was home to the Institute for the Eradication of Jewish Influence on German Church Life. Within the walls of Wartburg Castle some of Germany's finest biblical scholars would devote their talents to de-Judaizing the Bible. The Institute promulgated a theological rationale for *Kristallnacht* and is nowhere to be found in Bethge or Schlingensiepen.[58]

Also missing: Berlin-Grünewald's influence on Bonhoeffer's personality as well as attendant cultural forces of Weimar Germany; Dr. Karl Bonhoeffer's involvement in a Nazi-era eugenics consultation; Bonhoeffer's capacious and cosmopolitan sensibility and uncommonly generative encounters with Islam in Libya and Morocco; Bonhoeffer's direct and indirect criticisms of Barmen and Bethel; Bonhoeffer's immanent criticisms of Martin Luther on justification and the church; the unflattering truth of the Confessing Church's indifference to Jewish persecution.

Also missing in Schlingensiepen: any trace of Bonhoeffer's bodily existence, his affections, tastes, and sensibility.

Why doesn't Schlingensiepen mention Bonhoeffer's "great liberation from guilt and self-doubt" during his final year in prison? Why don't we learn of Bonhoeffer's discovery of *hilaritas*, the "boldness" possessed by Rembrandt, Michelangelo, the Knight of Bamberg, Luther, Lessing, Rubens, Hugo Wolf, Karl Barth, and even Friedrich Nietzsche, such that they held "the firm conviction that they are doing the world *good* with their work, even if the world isn't pleased with it"?[59]

---

58. It was, however, in Eisenach that Schlingensiepen delivered his first public rebuke of *Strange Glory*; in his lecture "Amerikanische Biografien vereinnahmen Bonhoeffer. Ein Blick auf Charles Marsh: A Life of Dietrich Bonhoeffer - mit einem Seitenblick auf das gegensätzliche Buch von Eric Metaxas," with his colleague Heiner Süselbeck. The occasion was the 2014 meeting of the German Section of the International Bonhoeffer Society. The lecture would appear in published form in the International Bonhoeffer Society *Rundbrief* (Nancy Lukens, correspondence with the author, September 11, 2014).

59. Bonhoeffer, *Letters and Papers*, 317.

Why is there nothing in Schlingensiepen on Bonhoeffer's view of abortion as murder, best read in the context of disagreements with his father on bioethics and natural life?

Why does Schlingensiepen trivialize Bonhoeffer's relationship with Reinhold Niebuhr, simplify the relationship with Barth, and ignore all his Jewish neighbors in Berlin-Grunewald? Why does he evade the question of Luther's antisemitism? There's not a single mention of the tract *On the Jews and Their Lies*—"Set fire to their synagogues and schools"—and its influence on the German Christians.[60]

Gesturing toward Schlingensiepen's criticism more broadly, a dimension of Bonhoeffer's story neglected in previous biographical accounts *is his originality as a thinker*. Thirty years ago, I wrote a doctoral dissertation on Bonhoeffer's early philosophical theology. When Oxford University Press accepted a revised version for publication, Bethge provided an endorsement for the hardback edition—"A theological sensation," he said. When I saw the full text in German, it floored me to realize that he had written the same phrase, "eine theologische Überraschung," that Barth had used to describe Bonhoeffer's doctoral dissertation *Sanctorum Communio*.

If Schlingensiepen demurs on Bonhoeffer's early philosophical writings, the late work he trivializes in a manner no less breezy than Metaxas.[61]

---

60. Martin Luther, *On the Jews and Their Lies*, trans. Martin H. Bertram, in *The Christian in Society IV*, ed. Franklin Sherman, Luther's Works (Philadelphia: Fortress, 1971) 47:123–307. See also David Turner, "Martin Luther: 'First Set Fire to Their Synagogues . . . That God Might See That We Are Christians,'" *Jerusalem Post*, October 9, 2014, https://www.jpost.com/blogs/the-jewish-problem---from-anti-judaism-to-anti-semitism/martin-luther-first-set-fire-to-their-synagogues-that-god-might-see-that-we-are-christians-378445.

61. In his widely cited review in the *Christian Century*, the distinguished scholar Clifford Green notes Metaxas's embarrassment with Bonhoeffer's ponderous ideas, such as "religionless Christianity" and other seemingly anomalous theological fragments written in prison writings. Green recalls that in a Trinity Forum interview Metaxas claimed Bonhoeffer "never really said [religionless Christianity]," but then Green writes, "[Metaxas] had to retract that because, well, Bonhoeffer did say it. But, Metaxas continues, he wrote it

These are powerful, and undeniably urgent, meditations that mark Bonhoeffer's theological daring and illuminate with astonishing prescience the entirely unfamiliar landscape on which Protestant thought landed in the wake of the Holocaust.

Bonhoeffer's late, fragmentary meditations on "religionless Christianity" trade, in some measure, on this forthright Reformed conviction: religion is based on humanity's search for God, but Christianity begins with God's reaching out to humankind. Religionless Christianity means, more prosaically, relationship with God without the entrapments of religion.[62]

Still, it is undeniable that aspects of Bonhoeffer's late meditations move in new and quite daring directions. "I am living, and can live, for days without the Bible," he said. "Authenticity, life, freedom, and mercy" acquired a new significance for him.[63]

Missing from Schlingensiepen's account is any appreciation of Bonhoeffer's intellectual powers in the history of modern thought, whereas I wanted to frame his prodigious imaginative powers within this story.

In the preface to his book *Antonioni: The Poet of Images*, the classicist William Arrowsmith pays tribute to Italian filmmaker Michelangelo Antonioni by placing him among the intellectual innovators of the twentieth century. "Let me be clear about what I think," Arrowsmith told an audience in 1977 at New York's Museum of Modern Art, "Antonioni is one of the greatest living artists, and as a director of film, his only living peer is Kurosawa; and he is unmistakably the peer of the other great masters in all the arts.

privately in a letter to Bethge and never intended anyone to see it because it was 'utterly out of keeping with the rest of Bonhoeffer's life.' He calls Bonhoeffer's theological prison reflections a 'few bone fragments . . . set upon by famished kites and less noble birds, many of whose descendants gnaw them still.'" See Clifford Green, "Hijacking Bonhoeffer," *Christian Century*, October 4, 2010, https://www.christiancentury.org/reviews/2010-09/hijacking-bonhoeffer.

62. Bonhoeffer, *Letters and Papers*, 366–67.

63. Bonhoeffer quoted in Lisa E. Dahill, "Bringing Voice to Life: Bonhoeffer's Spirituality in Translation," in *Interpreting Bonhoeffer: Historical Perspective, Emerging Issues*, ed. Clifford J. Green and Guy C. Carter (Minneapolis, MN: Fortress, 2013) 84.

As an innovator and manipulator of images, he is the peer of Joyce in the novel; in creating a genuine cinematic poetry, he stands on a level with Valéry and Eliot in poetry proper; and that his artistic vision, while perhaps no greater than that of Fitzgerald or Eliot or Montale or Pavese, is at least as great and compelling."[64] The same could be said of Bonhoeffer's body of work; his capacious intellectual powers and innovations in theological style inspired me to cast him as one of the most original thinkers of the modern age.

Schlingensiepen's criticisms canter on. I was "very mistaken," he writes, to say that Bonhoeffer's teaching at Finkenwalde would be illegal as a result of the Gleichschaltung of the Protestant Church. Did I not know that the

> Reich Church never had anything to do with Finkenwalde, the seminary for training clergy, a seminary which had been founded by the Confessing Church. Nor could any church withdraw Bonhoeffer's "*venia legendi*," his authority to teach. Only the Prussian Minister for Culture could do that, as an act of state. It was he who withdrew Bonhoeffer's *venia legendi* in 1936, when the Minister for the Reich Church had already declared all seminaries of the Confessing Church illegal a year earlier. This was done in 1935, at the insistence of the SS.[65]

Not a fatal mistake at all: these annotations fit fine with my general observation that Bonhoeffer's tenure as the theological director at Finkenwalde remained dissident in the eyes of the Reich's Church, exactly because Finkenwalde was a seminary of the Confessing Church, whose activity had been declared illegal. I do not make any claims regarding the withdrawal of Bonhoeffer's "authority to teach," and there can hardly be any doubt as to the "camp" Bonhoeffer belonged to. The lectures comprising the core of the Finkenwalde curriculum would not be published until 1937, after the seminary had been shut down. Karl Barth, we might recall, famously wrote in the final section of the *Church Dogmatics*

---

64. Arrowsmith, *Antonioni: The Poet of Images*, ed. Ted Perry (New York: Oxford University Press, 1995) 4.

65. Schlingensiepen, "Making Assumptions about Dietrich."

that as he turned his attention to a theology of discipleship, he was inclined to do no more than reproduce long passages from Bonhoeffer's account and let the matter stand at that. We know the book as *Nachfolge*, translated in the *Dietrich Bonhoeffer Works* as *Discipleship*, though in the United States more often read under the title *The Cost of Discipleship*, an austere meditation on the church in extremis. The will to make oneself an exemplar of faith could become too easily a recipe for a tortured soul or, worse, for an unforgiving perfectionism and sanctimonious bravado. But these were the right words spoken at the right time, when only a rare ardor and rectitude, deliberate discipline concentrated on the way of the cross, could save the church. The promise for those who follow Christ is that "they will become members of the community of the cross"—indeed "people of the mediator, people linked together by the cross, and thus by a way that leads to suffering."[66] Finkenwalde was the experiment in "new monasticism" that Bonhoeffer had mentioned in a 1935 letter to his brother Karl-Friedrich. It's a remarkable letter in which we see Bonoheffer laboring to explain the "fanatic" and "mad" zeal for Jesus that had overtaken him—and that perplexed members of his family.[67]

66. Bonhoeffer, *DBWE: Discipleship*, eds. Geoffrey Kelly and John Godsey, trans. Reinhard Krauss and Barbara Green (Minneapolis: Fortress, 2003) 4:99.

67. Bonhoeffer wrote, "Perhaps I seem to you rather fanatical and mad about a number of things. I myself am sometimes afraid of that. But I know that the day I became more 'reasonable,' to be honest, I should have to chuck my entire theology. "When I first started in theology, my idea of it was quite different—rather more academic, probably. Now it has turned into something else altogether. But I do believe that at last I am on the right track, for the first time in my life. I often feel quite happy about it. I only worry about being so afraid of what other people will think as to get bogged down instead of going forward. I think I am right in saying that I would only achieve true inner clarity and honesty by really starting to take the Sermon on the Mount seriously.

"Here alone lies the force that can blow all this hocus-pocus sky-high—like fireworks, leaving only a few burnt-out shells behind. The restoration of the church must surely depend on a new kind of monasticism, which has nothing in common with the old but a life of uncompromising discipleship, following Christ according to the Sermon on the Mount. I believe the time has come to gather people together and do this" (Letter to Karl-Friedrich Bonhoeffer, January 14, 1935, in Bonhoeffer, *DBWE: London*, ed. Keith W. Clements, trans.

In service to story and character, it was my intent to tread lightly over the thorny road of German Lutheran history, giving the reader details in tolerable doses. "The thing that is necessarily overlooked," Wallace Stevens writes, "is the presence of the determining personality."[68] Indifferent to character, Schlingensiepen's biography is instead a mountainous shoveling-on of facts that could have easily buried the reader alive. And in the end, his "Theses Against the American Marsh's *Roman* [Novel]" notwithstanding, he agrees with the logic of method: "The fate of the 'German Protestant Church' in Hitler's Germany will interest very few people in Germany today."[69] His interminable disputations on Lutheran polity in the German Protestant Church from 1933 to 1939 are the rattle of a peacock's train.

Without a principle of selectivity, the narrative sprawls endlessly; selectivity keeps the story focused and the biographer sane. It's important to be honest about this point, even though it's plainly obvious. A writer can aspire toward mastery of his subject and encyclopedic breadth. Closer to home, Dumas Malone wrote a six-volume "definitive" account of Thomas Jefferson but was no less bound to the principle of selectivity than had he packed it all into a Penguin Lives.[70] He would not have disagreed. Still, Malone's

Isabel Best [Minneapolis: Fortress, 2007] 13:284–85.

In the first decade of the twenty-first century, some readers might recall, the term *new monasticism* came much in vogue among certain North American practitioners of Christian community, many of whom were explicitly influenced by Bonhoeffer's writings at Finkenwalde. Bonhoeffer, though, was not the first to speak of a new monasticism. Perhaps he heard the term first from Niebuhr, who was writing, as early as 1926, of how he had become convinced— as a pastor-theologian in Henry Ford's Detroit and in a nation "engulfed in American luxury"—that "what we need is a 'new kind of monasticism' that restores a sense of tension between the soul and its environment" (Niebuhr cited in Richard Fox, *Reinhold Niebuhr: A Biography* [New York: Pantheon, 1985] 66).

68. Stevens quoted in Edward Ragg, *Wallace Stevens and the Aesthetics of Abstraction* (New York: Cambridge University Press, 2010) 116.

69. Schlingensiepen, "Making Assumptions about Dietrich."

70. Dumas Malone, *Jefferson and His Time*, 6 vols. (Charlottesville, VA: University of Virginia Press, 1948–81); Frank Shuffelton, "Being Definitive: Jefferson Biography under the Shadow of Dumas Malone," *Biography* 18, no.

three thousand pages give the reader no reason to think that Jefferson's relationship to his slaves was anything other than genteel patriarchy.

Had subsequent accounts of Jefferson's life adhered to Malone's evasion of the black and white bodies, the discovery of his sexual relationship with his enslaved, sixteen-year-old mistress, Sally Hemings, and the children they had together, as well as his imperious, often brutal treatment of the African Americans in his possession would have gone unnoticed, and the "master" of Monticello would have remained the uncontested moral arbiter of his academical village.[71]

"One only has to follow Eberhard Bethge's great biography," Schlingensiepen declares. "Metaxas has followed this more closely than Marsh, which is why he is more reliable."[72] And with a stroke of the pen, he becomes the only Bonhoeffer scholar in the world with a favorable impression of Eric Metaxas.

III. No New Research

Schlingensiepen then unveils a criticism that he thinks will be the coup de grâce. "Both authors are said to have included new research," he writes. The other author is Metaxas. "Whereas Metaxas actually presents very little that is new in this respect," he continues, "New findings are restricted to the chapter on Bonhoeffer's first visit to the United States in Marsh's book."[73]

4 (1995): 291.

71. See Annette Gordon-Reed's groundbreaking book *Thomas Jefferson and Sally Hemings: An American Controversy* (Charlottesville, VA: University of Virginia Press, 1997). Importantly, the historian Fawn Brodie was the first biographer to take the Hemings allegation seriously in her 1974 *Thomas Jefferson: An Intimate History* (New York: Norton) which received hard condemnation at the time for it—by Malone and others. Gordon-Reed acknowledges Brodie's efforts. Likewise, I'm grateful to the brilliant young historian Isaac Barnes May for these observations regarding Jefferson scholarship.

72. Schlingensiepen, "Making Assumptions about Dietrich."

73. "It is true that his book surpasses that of Bethge in terms of writerly skill," Schlingensiepen continues. "There were two passages that we read with

This is a scurrilous and incoherent claim. He earlier deemed *Strange Glory* unreliable because it strays from Bethge's account—and thus his own—and now he asserts that my biography is uninformative because it lacks new research.

What then is the provenance of its 515 pages?

Schlingensiepen is correct to say that I originally planned to write a book on Bonhoeffer in America. Experiences and encounters of Bonhoeffer's postdoctoral year at Union Theological Seminary (from 1930 to 1931) and the tumultuous six weeks, back in New York, in summer 1939, would be the lens through which I would tell the story. Books such as *Nietzsche in Turin*, *Adorno in America*, and *The Death of Sigmund Freud* (set in London) appealed to my interest in observing transformations of character under the constraints of unfamiliar places.

It vexed me to learn, however, that in his investigations into the origins of *Strange Glory*, he obtained a copy of the 2007 book proposal that I had written for my literary agent, and which she in turn submitted to trade and academic publishers, and that, undaunted by legal proprieties,[74] he mined the proposal to craft sentences like the following: "I remember a passage about him wanting to approach the topic in a more 'writerly' way than Bethge, using a talent for storytelling for which the Southern States are famous.

---

great interest, with admiration indeed: (1) His accounts of the two earlier books by Bonhoeffer (*Sanctorum Communio* und *Akt und Sein*) are very good. (Metaxas did not engage with these texts at all and dismissed the 'neue Theologie' from Tegel); (2) Marsh's chapter on Bonhoeffer's first sojourn in the US is excellent. One learns new insights and trusts Marsh that Bonhoeffer's experiences in the US had a more profound impact on his life than we could have known until now. (Even in the Metaxas book, this chapter is almost tolerable; but Marsh's account is distinctly better). But Marsh's account has become 'A Life of Bonhoeffer' that never existed in this form."

74. The title page of the proposal includes an unambiguous assignment of claim: "No addressee should forward, print, copy, or otherwise reproduce this message in any manner that would allow it to be viewed by any individual not originally listed as a recipient. If the reader of this message is not the intended recipient, you are hereby notified that any unauthorized disclosure, dissemination, distribution, copying, or the taking of any action in reliance on the information herein is strictly prohibited. If you have received this communication in error, please immediately notify the sender and delete this message."

At the closing of his rather elaborate text, [Marsh] wrote that he felt he was born to write this book. Without trying to be ironic, we wish for him to be on this earth for something more worthwhile than this very strange 'Life of Dietrich Bonhoeffer.'"[75]

But Schlingensiepen was right about the initial design. Bonhoeffer's two visits to the United States offered me all the elements of compelling nonfiction narrative.

The first, as a visiting student at Union Theological Seminary in New York for the academic year beginning in 1930, was a singularly transformative period. He arrived in Manhattan a straight-arrow, twenty-five-year-old philosophical theologian with two doctoral dissertations under his belt. The trip was kind of a lark for him, something to pass his time. But when he left New York ten months later, he'd discovered a new way of thinking about the theological vocation. In these unfamiliar worlds of American social theology, progressive Protestant organizing, and African American cultural and religious life—in "the church of the outcasts of America"—he reexamined his Germanic academic training in theology and ministry and embarked upon "the turning from the phraseological to the real," as he would observe. "It was the problem of concreteness that at present so occupies me," he later wrote.[76]

It excited me as a student of the American civil rights movement to learn of Bonhoeffer's road trip in the spring of 1931, a four-thousand-mile, seven-week journey that took him through the Deep South during the most harrowing years of Jim Crow segregation. His impressions of the trip, with studied observations of race relations, appear in the year-end report to his supervisor; he writes of "blood laws," "mob rule," "sterilizations," and "land seizures." He told his brother Karl-Friedrich that Germany would need an ACLU of its own.[77]

75. Ferdinand Schlingensiepen and Heiner Süselbeck, "American Biographies Co-opt Bonhoeffer: Looking at Charles Marsh's A Life of Dietrich Bonhoeffer with a Brief Glance at the Contrasting Book by Eric Metaxas," the International Dietrich Bonhoeffer Group Rundbrief, 2014.

76. Bonhoeffer quoted in Marsh, Strange Glory, 134.

77. Marsh, Strange Glory, 121–25.

Within two years of returning to Germany, the Nuremburg laws were passed. And within weeks of their passage in 1933 and the codification of anti-Jewish church policies in the so-called Aryan paragraph, Bonhoeffer explained to a group of Lutheran pastors that it was the obligation of the church not simply to bandage the victims under the wheel of state violence, whether these victims were Christian or not, but to crush the wheel itself.

But as I mentioned above, I soon realized that the American experiences would need a before, between, and after, by which time I'd be on the way to a cradle-to-grave account.

In criticizing *Strange Glory* for a lack of new research, Schlingensiepen falls back on his favorite hobbyhorse. Every biographer of Bonhoeffer must "acquire a thorough knowledge of the German Protestant church during this time," apart from which "a description of . . . . Bonhoeffer's life will fail."[78]

In leveling these charges against me, Schlingensiepen again invites criticisms of his biography. He gives the reader four soporific pages on Bonhoeffer's year in Barcelona (1927–28) for the reason that, as he says, "Bonhoeffer's encounter with Spanish Catholicism was a bitter disappointment to him." The opposite is true.

It must be difficult for a born-in-the-wool Lutheran clergyman from the provinces to fathom Bonhoeffer's cosmopolitan sensibilities. Bonhoeffer found Spanish Catholicism positively thrilling. He marveled at how his thinking had taken a humanistic turn. The pageantry of sun and sea illuminated for him a new field of vision. He felt that "a theology of . . . spring and summer" was replacing "the Berlin winter theology," that his theology "was becoming more humanistic." He pondered the question, cited earlier—and what a marvelous question it is, worthy of an international congress of its own—whether "Karl Barth could have written in Spain."[79]

78. Schlingensiepen, "Making Assumptions about Dietrich."

79. Bonhoeffer quoted in Andreas Pangritz, *Karl Barth in the Theology of Dietrich Bonhoeffer*, trans. Barbara Rumscheidt and Martin Rumscheidt, 2nd ed. (Eugene, OR: Wipf & Stock, 2000) 24.

The Barcelona year deserves a chapter of its own, and in *Strange Glory* it got just that: chapter 4, "Greetings from the Matador" (pp. 62–88), was based on my research in Spain and at the Lutheran congregation of Barcelona, where Bonhoeffer served, on primary sources, and on Bethge's biography. The sermons read like lyrical essays; I count them among his most beautiful writings. A mystical current guides the pen. It's possible to see everything already in these homilies, which can't be said at all for his three public lectures in Barcelona. And that these sermonic essays followed the doctoral dissertation *Sanctorum Communio* so closely gives them the sense of being little miracles.

At times Bonhoeffer seems to be riffing on Barth's *Das Wort Gottes und die Theologie* and its expressionist energies, but with a mystical dimension.

A rundown of the new research and biographical perspectives coalescing into *Strange Glory* would require an inventory taken of each chapter and page. By my estimation, 70 percent of the content has not appeared in any previous biography. Common sense alone would suggest the statistical improbability of Schlingensiepen's claim that I wrote my narrative without relying on Bethge while simultaneously using no new material.

IV. Hero Worship

In claiming that I put Bonhoeffer on a pedestal and treat him "as if he were the sole opponent of Hitler," Schlingensiepen left me questioning his ability to read and interpret written communication. I do not mean to add snark, to snipe and sink to ad hominem attacks myself. I wish only to convey my initial response to a criticism so patently false.

In chapters 8 through 13, I cover the numerous measures put in place against ministers and members of Confessing Church congregations, including details on Bonhoeffer's imprisoned friends, students, and fellow ministers who were opposed to the Nazi regime. I devote an entire chapter to Bonhoeffer's years as the director of Finkenwalde and training of non-Nazi pastors. Dozens of church dissidents and political conspirators number among the dramatic personae of *Strange Glory* and are included by name. But I wanted my telling of Bonhoeffer's role in the conspiracy against Hitler to be more than a montage of historical plaques.

Nevertheless, what seems to agitate Schlingensiepen is my unwillingness to join his panegyric to the "actually large number of men and women in the Confessing Church . . . who fought as courageously or maybe even more courageously than did Bonhoeffer . . . [and] remained principled opponents of National Socialism until the end."[80] This kind of work falls outside the scope of a written life, and as I noted earlier, it's not a statement that I recognize as truthful.

By "principled," Schlingensiepen would appear to mean "opponents in principle," invoking again the ecclesial-theological language of the Confessing Church. If you assent to Barmen, Bethel, and Dahlem, Schlingensiepen infers your opposition to National Socialism. Except the inference does not contain the political judgment. Does he intend the phrase "opponents of National Socialism" to mean opponents of the Nazi genocide of the Jewish people?[81] If so, he's fudging the truth.

In any case, Bonhoeffer knew well that the Confessing Church refused to speak a concrete word against the Nazi genocide of the Jewish people. And his realization that it never would is one of the narrative threads running through his decision to leave Germany in the summer of 1939 for his second trip to America. Bethge called this thread the "lure of the political."

When ministers of the Confessing Church met on June 11, 1938, for their final disputation on "the Jewish question," it depressed Bonhoeffer to learn that the majority had taken the oath of

80. Schlingensiepen, "Making Assumptions about Dietrich."

81. It's worth remembering that such Confessing Church leaders as Martin Niemöller spoke eloquently in defense of Christians of Jewish descent ("non-Aryans") but remained theologically indifferent, if not contemptuous towards religious Jews. There's good reason to be skeptical of the many accounts of the Kirchenkampf in which the Confessing Church's defense of Christians of Jewish descent is used as a synecdochic placeholder for its witness against the Holocaust.

CHARLES MARSH

allegiance to Hitler. According to Bethge: 60 percent of the ministers in Rhineland swore allegiance, 70 percent in Brandenburg, 78 percent in Saxony, 80 percent in Pomerania, 82 percent in Silesia, and 89 percent in Grenzmark.[82]

Schlingensiepen's claim that I bathe Bonhoeffer in saintly bliss is absurd, and it should not distract us from the real purpose of his deceptive stunt: to skew the historical record so as to portray the Confessing Church as heroic opponents of Hitler. The effect of his encomium to good German churchmen such as his father, Hermann Schlingensiepen, who trained Lutheran pastors for mission work in South America, is a confused and misleading portrayal of Bonhoeffer's singular dissent. And it leads him to the preposterous claim that Bonhoeffer remained "untroubled by the Nazi regime while in Finkenwalde."[83]

Bonhoeffer made mistakes of judgment and knew it. He intoned the "bold venture of faith" but often felt immobilized by uncertainty. "I just cannot see how to get things right," Bonhoeffer says on the eve of Hitler's ascent to power.[84] Still, he discerned in the appointment of Hitler as chancellor in 1933 the emergence of "the great masquerade of evil." What enabled this perception? This question forms the characterological arc from the child's first perceptions in Breslau to the conspirator's last prayer at Flossenbürg.

V. The Question of Bonhoeffer's Sexual Orientation

Schlingensiepen's criticisms of my book finally land on my portrayal of Bonhoeffer's relationship with Bethge. No surprise here: you kind of knew this was where he was heading all along.

Schlingensiepen is aghast that I even broached the subject of Bonhoeffer's sexual orientation. Any hypothesis in this vein is "completely unfounded," he says, although he knows, as an active member of the International Bonhoeffer Society, that Bonhoeffer's

82. Bethge, *Dietrich Bonhoeffer*, 601.

83. Schlingensiepen, "Making Assumptions about Dietrich."

84. Bonhoeffer, *No Rusty Swords: Letters, Lectures and Notes 1928–1936*, ed. Edwin H. Robertson (New York: Harper & Row) 123–24.

sexuality has long been discussed. I can recall a half dozen occasions when the subject arose in lively exchange over meals or drinks at conferences. No one was aghast, especially those who had worked closely on the later editions of the *Dietrich Bonhoeffer Works*. The only shock my book registered among Bonhoeffer scholars was that of recognition—the open secret explored in narrative.[85]

But Schlingensiepen dodges the textual evidence in *Strange Glory* for Bonhoeffer's homoerotic affections, dismissing my

---

85. Schlingensiepen, "Making Assumptions about Dietrich." This might explain Barnett's umbrage in her August 2014 "Letter to the Editor" in the *New York Times*, shared with the author in an email on August 11: "To the editor: The dangers of how quickly speculation can become accepted fact are apparent in several recent reviews of Charles Marsh's Strange Glory: *A Life of Dietrich Bonhoeffer*, but when a respected scholar like Randall Balmer blithely repeats such speculation as truth in the *Times Book Review* someone needs to speak up. As one of the general editors of the English edition of the *DBWE*, I would emphasize that Marsh's portrayal of the relationship between Dietrich Bonhoeffer and his friend and colleague Eberhard Bethge as a homoerotic one is speculation, based upon Marsh's reading of the letters between the two men. It may be true, but we don't know for certain. I will say personally that I was troubled by Marsh's portrayal of this relationship in its initial phase, which does indeed read as if there were an active homosexual relationship between the two men, and I don't think there was. While Marsh backpedals later in the book, describing it more cautiously as 'chaste' and one-sided, the general impression given is the one Balmer repeats. Eberhard Bethge was not just a student, he became Bonhoeffer's right-hand man in overseeing the training of Confessing church seminarians, particularly after Bonhoeffer was limited by Gestapo restrictions, and Bethge was also active in the resistance circles. Perhaps most importantly, Bonhoeffer found Bethge to be a reliable sounding board and theological conversation partner and tasked him with completing his unfinished theological writings. This was indeed a remarkably close friendship and a very multifaceted one between equals. None of us knows whether it was more than a close friendship between Bonhoeffer and the man who became the executor of his literary estate. I wish that Professor Marsh in what is in many ways a fine book had acknowledged the speculative nature of his conclusions on this point." Note that the version published in the *New York Times* was heavily revised: "Letters: 'Bonhoeffer, Bethge and Hitler,'" *New York Times*, August 22, 2014, https://www.nytimes.com/2014/08/24/books/review/letters-a-troublesome-inheritance.html.

portrayal as a scheme to focus attention onto "the conflict between the Conservatives and the gay rights' [*sic*] movement."[86]

I approached the subject of Bonhoeffer and Bethge's seven-year friendship cautiously and with close attention to primary sources. I can confirm on the basis of correspondence with readers, book talks, and lectures that most readers of *Strange Glory* find my approach scrupulous to a fault.

An exchange with my editor at Knopf in the final months of writing offers a glimpse into my circumspect handling of Bonhoeffer's sexuality.

"It is not my intention to out Bonhoeffer," I wrote. "Bonhoeffer allows in a letter from prison that he never experienced the pleasures of sexual union. I take that as a truthful revelation; and because I believe him—he is writing to Eberhard and knows now he will die in a few months—it is my challenge to reconstruct his homoerotic attraction to Eberhard in its singular and storied particularity."[87]

What tipped the scales for me was the discovery of Bonhoeffer's letters to Bethge, written between November 1940 and February 1941. Here we find the most moving, eloquent, and heartbreaking evidence of Bonhoeffer's desire that he and Bethge might be united in something like a spiritual marriage until that day when they would "worship together for eternity."[88]

I can imagine the exchange existing as a stand-alone volume, *Love Letters from the Hotel Ludwig der Bayer*, published by a small literary press in a handsome edition with deckle edge and French flaps. Has no one but the editor and translator read them? Did the editors and translators of the *Dietrich Bonhoeffer Works* expect no one to notice?

---

86. Schlingensiepen, "Making Assumptions about Dietrich."

87. "I've already seen and experienced more of life than you have," Bonhoeffer wrote to a recently wedded Eberhard, "except for one crucial experience that you have, which I still lack—but perhaps that's precisely why I have already had more of 'my fill of life' than you as yet" (Bonhoeffer, *Letters and Papers*, 402).

88. See Bonhoeffer, *Conspiracy and Imprisonment*, 80–164.

In Ettal, Bonhoeffer experienced great loneliness during this unavoidable separation from Bethge, who was fulfilling pastoral duties at the Burckhardthaus in Berlin-Dahlem. Bonhoeffer had come to Ettal for the sanctuary it offered—and in hopes of writing his *Ethics*. The gestapo's recent charge against him for "activities subverting the people" and the prohibition from public speaking would soon be extended to his "every activity as a writer." By the time he left, he had completed major sections on "ultimate and penultimate things" and had "crafted a robust affirmation of the nature and the integrity of all created life."[89] The book would remain his unfinished masterpiece.

As the day light hours grew shorter, Bonhoeffer became desperate in his hope that Bethge would join him for Christmas in Ettal. The two would then go on holiday together to the Bonhoeffers' country house in the eastern Harz Mountains. Their separation felt "unnatural," he writes in a letter to Bethge.

Bonhoeffer passed his time alone imagining their reunion. For two years, he and Bethge had shared a bank account and given gifts as a pair. Bethge kept the "household" accounts and paid their taxes, whereas Bonhoeffer made the decision on how to spend the money. In this capacity, Bonhoeffer sent Bethge his ideas for Christmas presents and all the reasons Bethge should accept his invitation. They would go to the monastery for the midnight mass but otherwise celebrate Christmas by themselves. They could sleep by the fire, read books aloud to each other, and play the piano at all hours. They could rise late and cross-country ski, if the weather turned clear (it would). A trail ran along the mountainside from Ettal to Oberammergau, but there were many options. Bonhoeffer was ecstatic when Bethge said yes. "So we will be together as before!" he said.[90]

John W. de Gruchy noticed. De Gruchy, one of the leading religious voices in the anti-apartheid movement and an internationally renowned scholar who taught until his retirement at the University of Cape Town, told journalist Sarah Pulliam Bailey in

89. Gestapo and Bonhoeffer quoted in Marsh, *Strange Glory*, 288 and 297.
90. Bonhoeffer quoted in Marsh, *Strange Glory*, 301.

2014 correspondence: "In writing my own biography of Eberhard Bethge, Bonhoeffer's closest friend, confidant and biographer, I arrived at the same conclusion about Bonhoeffer as has Charles [Marsh]. And like Charles I avoided saying that he was gay only because the word today sometimes conveys more than can be said about Bonhoeffer. Bethge was certainly not gay and there is not the slightest shred of evidence to suggest that his relationship with Dietrich was sexual. Theirs was a remarkable platonic friendship expressed so well in Bonhoeffer's poem 'The Friend' which he wrote with Bethge in mind. Bonhoeffer might well have been attracted to other males, but there is also no evidence at all that would suggest anything more than attraction."[91]

In his review of my book, Schlingensiepen ignores the Ettal correspondence. The only evidence he brings to the question is a letter from Bethge recalling a time in "1957/58" when he was asked the nature of his relationship with Bonhoeffer. Bethge writes the following:

> During a large student convention in a snow-covered New Hampshire 1957/58. Someone asked me who the other correspondent had been, since they must have been homosexuals given the intimate and intense correspondence. No, we were rather normal. Of course today, one knows that every same-sex friendship carries an element of homoeroticism. But for us, the reason we were so close from the beginning was simply that Dietrich had severed the relationship to a woman that had lasted for several years and confided in me during this painful process. At the same time, I had reached the bitter end of an engagement, an experience I shared with him. On the other hand, it was the case that our friendship, towards the end, had led both of us into relationships with very vivacious new partners, whose developments and

91. Correspondence from De Gruchy to Marsh and Sarah Pulliam Bailey for publication. A portion of this was quoted in Bailey, "Was Dietrich Bonhoeffer Gay? A New Biography Raises Questions," *Washington Post*, July 3, 2014, https://www.washingtonpost.com/national/religion/was-dietrich-bonhoeffer-gay-a-new-biography-raises-questions/2014/07/03/5557f47e-02e8-11e4-866e-94226a02bc8d_story.html.

whose difficulties caused by the war, we shared with each other, in the way that men do, before anyone else comes to know of these things. . . . Both of our love stories were indeed normal. And they were full of intensity, even if the forms of expression could be considered prude by to-day's standards. Meanwhile, we had already understood the Song of Solomon back then.[92]

This appeal to an exchange that took place twelve years after Germany's unconditional surrender—in which Schlingensiepen translates "We were rather normal" as "We were actually pretty straight"—is a convenient way to dismiss questions about Bonhoeffer's sexuality. But Bethge's fascinating elliptical and exceedingly awkward reverie does not close the book on all present and future questions about Bonhoeffer's sexuality. It's also worth mentioning that in 1958, when Bethge wrote that paragraph, homosexuality remained both illegal and taboo in Germany and the United States alike. If Bethge had believed Bonhoeffer was sexually attracted to him, it would have damaged Bonhoeffer's legacy at the time to say as much.[93]

Ettal gets a heavy Lutheran gloss in Schlingensiepen, while *Strange Glory* devotes a full chapter to Bonhoeffer's snowbound winter as a guest of the Benedictine monks in the Klosterstadt eighty miles south of Munich.

My narrative forays into Bonhoeffer's "secret passion" so vex Schlingensiepen that even my attention to Bonhoeffer's sartorial flamboyance is taken as another manipulative turn in my outing.[94] What is wrong with flamboyance, one might ask? Unless flamboyance in men reproduces homophobic stereotypes and flamboyance is unmanly and therefore gay?

92. Bethge, "Mein Freund Dietrich Bonhoeffer," in *Theologie und Freundschaft: Wechselwirkungen, Eberhard Bethge und Dietrich Bonhoeffer*, ed. Christian Gremmels and Wolfgang Huber (Gütersloh, Germany: Chr. Kaiser/ Gütersloher Verlaghaus, 1994) 15.

93. I am indebted to Isaac Barnes May for bringing the obvious to my attention.

94. Schlingensiepen, "Making Assumptions about Dietrich."

Schlingensiepen's indifference to bodily and natural life might be excusable in histories of ecclesial institutions, but in a written life, the consequences are grave. "All knowledge is mixed up with what goes on in human minds and in the sentences that inform our body and give shape to our being," Leon Edel writes.[95] Instead of the luminous bon vivant who leaps off the pages of his letters and papers, we're given a Lutheran churchman bereft of passion. Schlingensiepen's evasion of human sexuality is the erasure of Bonhoeffer's body.[96]

Karl Barth once said: "Not everything, but a great deal in the phenomenon of man both individually and more generally may, in fact, be explained by the fact that we are continually hungry, sexually unsettled, and in need of sleep." Barth warned Christians that "life is conditioned by the necessity of metabolism and by sexuality."[97]

Out of loyalty to an ideal of Christian manhood unfamiliar to either Barth or Bonhoeffer, Schlingensiepen warns intrepid biographers against speaking of Barth's body. My passing remark that Barth's relationship with Charlotte von Kirschbaum was not—as Schlingensiepen and most Barth scholars spent a half century arguing—merely Platonic is "intrusive" and "incorrect." He says that "one is tempted to modify Talleyrand's saying: 'It is not only heresy, it is worse for it is bad taste.' (If one should truly include Paul Tillich's sexual escapades (450 f.) in a biography on Bonhoeffer is a different question altogether.)"[98]

95. Edel, "Figure under the Carpet," 22.

96. This stance is hardly unique. In his 2018 doctoral thesis at the University of Cambridge, "A Friendship for Others: Bonhoeffer and Bethge on the Theology and Practice of Friendship," Preston Parsons draws potential historical connections between Bonhoeffer's sexual orientation and what Weimar's gay community called *Freundschaft*, or intimate same-sex military friendships. But Parsons demurs on the question of bodily desire and homosexual affection, thus following other scholars in decoupling intellectual and embodied intimacy (142–44).

97. Barth, *Ethics*, ed. Dietrich Braun, trans. Geoffrey W. Bromiley (Eugene, OR: Wipf & Stock, 2013; first published in English 1981 by Seabury) 128.

98. Schlingensiepen and Süselbeck, "American Biographies Co-opt Bonhoeffer."

Schlingensiepen's scold is an embarrassment. Did he not get the memo?

Let me explain.

After his expulsion from Germany in 1935, Barth would pass the remainder of his career in Switzerland, attended by his loyal wife, Nelly, and his strikingly beautiful assistant, Kirschbaum, or Lollo as he called her, who came to occupy a room in the professor's home. The two women resided under the same roof with the famous theologian triangulating the upstairs bedrooms according to terms deemed necessary to complete his great *Church Dogmatics*. He referred to the arrangement as a *Notgemeinschaft* ("emergency community").

Until 2017 the principals of Barth, Inc., were no less punishing than the Bonhoeffer guild to the occasional scholar or theologian insinuating that the Karl-Charlotte pairing involved more than shared doctrine and deep work. Various shifting and increasingly implausible explanations were proffered. One defense, popularly attributed to the distinguished Yale theologian Hans Frei, described the relationship as Barth's "over-commitment to theology," which is vague enough to mean anything, so let's give Professor Frei the last laugh on this line of defense.[99]

More typical among the Barth epigones were variations on the theme of going about his sacred duties with the kindly aid of a kindred soul. From the time the two first shared a house together in February 1926, Kirschbaum "committed herself . . . to doing everything she possibly could to advance theological work," writes George Hunsinger, a professor at Princeton Theological Seminary and founder/director of the Karl Barth Center. In October 1925, Barth had joined the theology faculty in Münster, while his wife Nelly and their five small children remained in Göttingen until the end of the school year. At his request, Kirschbaum joined Barth for the month of February in Münster. "Unique student, critic, researcher, advisor, collaborator, companion, assistant,

---

99. This anecdote was shared with me by James J. Buckley, a former colleague and convivial conversation partner at Loyola University in Maryland, who studied with Professor Frei at Yale University in the 1970s.

spokesperson, and confidant [but not lovers] Charlotte von Kirsch-baum was indispensable to him."[100] So the story goes.

All the fraternal defenses imploded in 2017, when Christiane Tietz, a professor of theology at the University of Zurich, addressed the Karl Barth Society of North America at the annual meeting of the American Academy of Religion. The topic of her lecture was Barth's relationship with his wife and Kirschbaum. Tietz brought with her an arsenal of documents from the recently released Barth papers in Basel and blew a hole in the platonic defense that was big enough to drive a BVB tram through.

Tietz told the story of how Barth and Kirschbaum fell in love and came to cohabit with Barth's wife Nelly in this (to use Stephen Plant's most excellent translation) "emergency mutual aid society."[101] Reconstructing their letters to dramatic effect in English, reading Tietz's paper and the letters of Karl and Charlotte made me sad that John Updike had died before *L'affaire Barth*; it might have inspired a better rendering of the theological life than his *Roger's Version* disappointment.

At first, I wasn't completely sure Schlingensiepen was being serious in claiming that my book is but the ideological opposite of Metaxas's, both complicit in co-opting Bonhoeffer for the American culture wars. His title read like a bad joke—"American Biographies Co-opt Bonhoeffer: Looking at Charles Marsh's: A Life of Dietrich Bonhoeffer with a Brief Glance at the Contrasting Book by Eric Metaxas." But he was dead serious, and it makes perfect sense.

Despite their differences, the yappy Trump loyalist of the Upper East Side (by way of Queens) and the bearded Lutheran parson from the Rhineland, these men unite in opposing any consideration of Bonhoeffer's same-sex desires.

100. Hunsinger, review of *Charlotte von Kirschbaum and Karl Barth: A Study in Biography and the History of Theology* by Suzanne Selinger, *Journal of Religion* 80.4 (2000) 685–87, http://barth2.ptsem.edu/index.php/Book_Reviews/Book_Review/charlotte-von-kirschbaum-and-karl-barth.

101. Plant, "When Karl Met Lollo: The Origins and Consequences of Karl Barth's Relationship with Charlotte von Kirschbaum," *Scottish Journal of Theology* 72.2 (2019) 127–45.

If Schlingensiepen were the wordsmith that Metaxas fancies himself to be, he might have also called my account, as Metaxas did, a "lode of queering."[102] Instead, he blandly protests, "Bonhoeffer would have been under constant strain, if this had been his sexual orientation. Bethge would have sensed something. There was never any suggestion of such tensions when Bethge talked about his time with Bonhoeffer." In joining hands with Metaxas, Schlingensiepen lends support to one of American evangelicalism's most obsessive homophobes, who is in recent months, if his Twitter account and public statements are any indication, a minister of white nationalist propaganda.[103]

Schlingensiepen's evasion of Bonhoeffer's homoeroticism becomes problematic when viewed in the context of Nazi Christian obsessions with masculinity. In fact, Bonhoeffer's sensibilities and desires subverted the Nazi ideals of masculine religiosity, which saw homosexuality as a perversion of the natural order, "alien to the species," and a threat to German society and National Socialist population policy goals.[104] Not only the shape of Bonhoeffer's

102. Eric Metaxas cited in Jon Ward, "My Email Exchange with Eric Metaxas," *Medium*, February 23, 2018. The exchange was prompted by Ward's unflattering profile of Metaxas in *Yahoo News* (Ward, "Author Eric Metaxas, Evangelical Intellectual, Chose Trump, and He's Sticking with Him," *Yahoo News*, February 23, 2018, https://www.yahoo.com/news/author-eric-metaxas-evangelical-intellectual-chose-trump-hes-sticking-100012875.html). The full quote is spectacular. According to Metaxas, I portray Bonhoeffer "as a lavender swell mincing and vogue-ing his way through the corridors of the Third Reich"; "as gayer-by-a-yard-of-tulle than Charles Nelson Reilly and Charles Busch combined." My queering of the Berlin theologian is an "intellectually hideous" distortion of "one of the bravest—and genuinely manliest—Christians of the last century."

103. Schlingensiepen, "Making Assumptions about Dietrich." For Metaxas's recent comments, see Michael Gerson, "No, Eric Metaxas, Jesus Wasn't White," *Washington Post*, August 3, 2020, https://www.washingtonpost.com/opinions/the-white-european-jesus-of-western-imagination-is-fiction/2020/08/03/e495f5de-d5cb-11ea-aff6-220dd3a14741_story.html; Jack Jenkins and Emily McFarlan Miller, "Eric Metaxas Confirms He Punched Protester, Says Protester Was to Blame," *Religion News Service*, September 1, 2020, https://religionnews.com/2020/09/01/eric-metaxas-protester-menaced-punch-video-trump-rnc/.

104. Flossenbürg, *Permanent Catalogue*, 299.

sensibilities and desires, but more importantly the qualities and practices of vulnerability, suffering, listening, compassion, marginality, private and intercessory prayer, central to Bonhoeffer's Christology and his own exuberant witness—they all form an immanent repudiation of Nazi ideology and Nazi theology.[105] In the sixteen-volume *Dietrich Bonhoeffer Works*, one finds not a single condemnation of homosexuality.

Neither Schlingensiepen nor Metaxas mentions the Nazi regime's campaign to eradicate homosexuality in Germany—and in one truly pathetic attempt of legerdemain, Metaxas recycles the rumor that top Nazis leaders were closeted gay men, further demonstrating their depravity and, wink wink, the depravity of the "gay agenda" as well. By contrast, Metaxas calls Bonhoeffer "one of the . . . genuinely manliest Christians of the last century," resisting even the most cursory exploration of psychology, ignoring all evidence leading to a different image, and without concern for how Nazi Christians promoted Aryan ideals of masculinity to advance a de-Judaized Christ.[106]

The German Christians remained the majority membership of the Lutheran Church after 1933 in its allegiance to Hitler and to the Third Reich. Nazi theologians claimed that God had chosen the German people to be a new holy race and abrogated Israel's covenant. In turn, German Christians spoke of a new kind of church, a strong and manly church—*eine männliche Kirche*. The image of suffering-servant Christianity offended the Nazi mind. "In a manly time of struggle," exclaimed one Nazi pastor at a

---

105. See Kristopher Norris, "Toxic Masculinity and the Quest for Ecclesial Legitimation," *Journal of the Society of Christian Ethics* 39.2 (2019) 319–38. Norris shows how Bonhoeffer's life, theology, ethics, and practice of friendship subverted the hard, hypermasculine ecclesiology of the Nazified German Christian churches, particularly through trust, vulnerability, and responsibility; Bonhoeffer "stretched the boundaries of what his contemporary German culture would have identified as conventionally masculine[,] granted him insight about the crisis infecting the German church, and cultivated solidarity with other vulnerable people" (338).

106. Eric Metaxas, "My Email Exchange with Yahoo News!," *Eric Metaxas*, March 7, 2018, https://ericmetaxas.com/blog/email-exchange-jon-ward-yahoo-news/.

Frankfurt rally, "one cannot get by with effeminate and sweet talk of peace." In this way, unmanly Christianity was much like Judaism, the quintessence of weakness. Only a manly Christ could empower the martial aspirations of the Aryan nation, the capacity "to fight ruthlessly, to exhibit hardness and heroism, [and] to follow orders with discipline and enthusiasm," to rule as stormtroopers of the church. Thus, "men too old or too young to be soldiers, homosexuals, and men unwilling or unable to fight did not fit the bill."[107]

Yet, Schlingensiepen writes: "Marsh does not seem to know that homosexuals in Germany were being sent to concentration camps."[108]

Let's pause here. If true—it's not—I would be guilty of staggering and consequential ignorance. Anyone reading Schlingensiepen's piece would be justified in doubting my competence and moral fitness. Instead, this claim had me reaching for the smelling salts.

In fact, neither Schlingensiepen nor Metaxas mentions that the Flossenbürg concentration camp, where Bonhoeffer was held the night before his execution, housed more than three hundred "homosexuals" interned under paragraph 175 of the Reich Criminal Code. According to the *Catalogue of the Permanent Exhibition*, seventy-nine gay men are known to have died in Flossenbürg.[109] Not until I visited the concentration camp on a cold weekend of sleet and high winds did I know that it was among the first to house a division of the Pink Triangle.

107. Doris Bergan, *Twisted Cross: The German Christian Movement in the Third Reich* (Chapel Hill, NC: University of North Carolina Press, 1996) 63, 72–73. Bergen shows that the Confessing Church was also tethered to masculine ideals.

108. Schlingensiepen, "Making Assumptions about Dietrich."

109. Among the survivors was the Vienna-born Josef Kohout, whose 1972 book, *The Men with the Pink Triangle* (written under the pseudonym Heinz Heger) "became a symbol in the struggle to gain recognition for the persecution of homosexuals under the National Socialist regime" ("Josef Kohout," Flossenbürg Concentration Camp Memorial, https://www.gedenkstaette-flossenbuerg.de/en/history/prisoners/josef-kohout). See Heinz Heger [Josef Kohout] *The Men with the Pink Triangle*, trans. David Fernbach (London: Gay Men's Press, 1980).

According to most sources, between five and fifteen thousand gay men were sent to concentration camps, where many were subject to forced sterilizations and castration. "Another estimated 35,000 men spent time in regular prisons," while the gestapo compiled the names of over 100,000 German and Austrian men in so-called "pink lists."[110]

Homosexuality was denounced as a perversion of the natural order—and a threat to German family values and National Socialism's population goals. Some Nazi doctors likened homosexuals to Jews: both were inherently unpatriotic, inhabiting a "state within a state." Both were "weak and deceitful," "servile yet power hungry." Both were "enemies of the Reich to be eliminated."[111]

The Nazi assault on same-sex relationships is highlighted in *Strange Glory* at precisely those places in the story where previous biographers (Schlingensiepen among them) have remained silent.

Against the vulgarians of the Holy Reich and their boast to be "the embodiment of all manliness," Bonhoeffer spoke of a Christ who sojourns in the world as a beggar among beggars, in places of exclusion and distress, "concealing himself in weakness . . . an outcast among the outcast, a sinner among sinners."[112] Bonhoeffer's theological and emotional sensibilities subverted the marauding, muscular, violent aspirations of Nazi Christianity. And named its God an idol.

VI. Conclusion

The question persists: What is this all about? What would drive someone to turn a virtue—the virtue of literary texture—into an abomination?

---

110. Holocaust Museum, 4; and Flossenbürg, *Permanent Catalogue*, 299.

111. Flossenbürg Concentration Camp Memorial, *Permanent Catalogue*, 299. The historian Isaac Barnes May pointed out to me that "people convicted of homosexuality also carried those convictions into the German Democratic Republic [East Germany] and Federal Republic of Germany [West Germany] an issue which no other group targeted by the Nazis dealt with."

112. Marsh, *Strange Glory*, 172.

A hatchet job can be a thrill—it can light up your brain like a club drug. A pleasure to read, it must feel great to write. But when the rush is gone, you may look up to see that it's you everyone's looking at, and there's crazy in your face.

I've lingered long enough over one angry Lutheran from the Rhineland, and the answer eludes me.

I do know this: A day is coming when a coterie of insouciant young scholars, unmoved by the old pieties, will rummage through Bonhoeffer's life, desires, and affections—possibly with the help of archival discoveries, the insights of queer theory, memory/post-memory studies, and psychoanalysis—and see Bonhoeffer again for the first time. On that day, the keepers of the house will retreat once again to the old defenses only now to discover no ground beneath their feet.

FINAL MUSINGS ON THEOLOGY AND BIOGRAPHY

The Bonhoeffer encountered in *Strange Glory* may seem unfamiliar, but it is a portrait shaped by the materials of historical life as I observed them.

If you visit the German Resistance Memorial Center in Berlin, you'll see a statue of a single individual with his hands bound in the stone courtyard of the Bendler Block.

This building complex was central to the National Socialist regime, the headquarters of the Army High Command, and the site of the July 20, 1944, attempt to overthrow the Reich. It was in this courtyard that the military officers involved in the July 20 conspiracy were executed that night. While Nazism commanded a fusion of wills into the collective, the artwork at the Resistance Memorial honors the conspiracy and conspirators as an expression of individuals of conscience; indeed, here as a solitary person.[113]

"The biographer truly succeeds if a distinct literary form can be found for the particular life," Edel observes in *Writing Lives*.[114]

Reviews of Schlingensiepen's biography in the major German newspapers *Die Zeit*, *NZZ*, and *FAZ* picked up on his reluctance to shed light on the "human" side of Bonhoeffer, a consequence of his lack of critical distance from Bethge's work. Bethge's biography has its own flaws and blind spots and, fifty years after publication, invites an independent and fresh interpretation. "Though subsequent Bonhoeffer scholars have complemented and filled out Bethge's interpretation," Fritz Stern and Elisabeth Siften acknowledge in their superb book *No Ordinary Men*, "they haven't much challenged it: after half a century one would welcome a new perspective on the subject by someone coming to the subject afresh."[115]

In a brief review in *Die Zeit*, Klaus Harpprecht—a prominent German writer and biographer of Thomas Mann—praises Schlingensiepen's volume as a reliable and generally accessible account, while informing readers not to expect an "ingenious literary achievement." The reviewer says he had hoped to understand the "aspects of [Bonhoeffer's] affections." Perhaps, he surmised, Schlingensiepen ignored character and other elements of story because he simply lacked the talent "to produce a literary, lively and nuanced biography." Perhaps too a "young literary talent will be up for this task in the future."[116]

---

113. Theologians who invoke Bonhoeffer to fortify an ecclesial-centric methodology do not understand the collision of historical realities and doctrinal commitments that changed his thinking on the church after 1938. What Bethge calls the "lure of the political" was prompted by "the collapse of the ecclesial." I explore these shifts in *Strange Glory*, 273, 313, and 334–39.

114. Edel, *Writing Lives*, 17.

115. Sifton and Stern, *No Ordinary Men*, 146.

116. Klaus Harpprecht, "Von der Radikalität des Glaubens. Dietrich Bonhoeffer, der wirkungsmächtigste unter den Theologen des 20.

The visage of a dandy saint swanning down Unter den Linden with a bouquet of flowers is simply unbearable.[117] But Bonhoeffer loved flowers. He praised the scent of Cuba's *buddleja* and morning glories; the sweet scent had floated over the terrace of his Havana guesthouse on a 1930 Christmastime trip, and Bonhoeffer luxuriated in the memory. He praised the "triumphant" bluebells of a south Texas springtime, the bluebells and wild rhododendrons that blanketed the German hill country as far as the eye could see. In his cell at Tegel prison, he placed flowers from his parents' garden on a cast iron table. He liked that the room he rented as a freshman in Tübingen was always adorned with fresh-cut flowers.

Jahrhunderts—eine Biografie," *Zeit Online*, December 8, 2005, https://www.zeit.de/2005/50/ST-Bonhoeffer/komplettansicht.

117. You will not find Bonhoeffer mincing down Unter den Linden in *Strange Glory* or anywhere that I know of, outside Eric Metaxas's imagination. But it is surely worth noting that on days when Bonhoeffer took the streetcar from the Halensee train station near his home to Berlin-Mitte, to attend or give lectures at the theology faculty near the Hegelplatz, were he walking on Unter den Linden, he would have passed the Moustache-Lounge, a gay bar at the corner of Gormannstrasse, or the Passage, a narrow pedestrian mall between Unter den Linden and Friedrichstrasse and meeting place for homosexuals. A directory and map of erotic and nighttime Berlin in the beguiling oversized volume *Panic: The Erotic World of Weimar Berlin* shows not only the ten most popular *Dielen* and cabarets for gay men but twenty-two "Girl-Culture" and lesbian venues (including the Oh la la!, which did not open its doors until six o'clock in the morning), six nudist societies, five "transvestite clubs," and Dr. Magnus Hirschfield's Institute of Sexuality—most a leisurely walk for anyone familiar with Berlin's vast well-lit streets. Many criticisms of my account of Bonhoeffer's sexuality trade on the notion that our age has degraded male friendships by its hermeneutical suspicion of every same-sex gesture and that we have consequently forgotten that there once was a time when men lavished their affections on other men in ways that no one considered gay. These criticisms are worthy of attention in their particular instances, but as a general observation about young men coming of age in Weimar Berlin, they are naive. No benighted prairie outpost, Bonhoeffer's Berlin was a cornucopia of sexual experimentation, often in full display, and his liberal father and mother both studied the new theories about human sexuality with keen interest; nowhere in his voluminous oeuvre, it is worth noting, does one find a condemnation of homosexuality.

In his journals from his trip to Rome during Holy Week 1924, he marveled at the "white-robed Jesuits" at the Chiesa del Gesù, swaying like a "sea of flowers." On the occasion of his twin sister's return from a holiday, he welcomes her home with a bouquet of flowers.

I think too of an eighteen-year-old Sophie Scholl writing to her boyfriend about a camping trip. The letter is found in the book, *At the Heart of the White Rose: Letters and Diaries of Hans and Sophie Scholl*, which I've just now pulled off the shelf. "Who would have thought it possible that a tiny little flower could preoccupy a person so completely that there simply wasn't room for any other thought, or that I could have turned into the earth, I liked it so much." The dissident student group she formed with her brother and for which she would be executed went by the name of the White Rose.[118]

In Schlingensiepen's biography you will not find flowers.

*   *   *

Bonhoeffer once said to Eberhard that it is exceedingly difficult to believe in God without a living example. Although he promised to elaborate in later correspondence—"I will write in more detail about 'example' in the NT—we have almost entirely lost track of

118. Bonhoeffer quoted in Marsh, *Strange Glory*, 202 and 30; Sophie Scholl quoted in Richard Gillman, preface to Hans Scholl, *At the Heart of the White Rose: Letters and Diaries of Hans and Sophie Scholl* (Walden, NY: Plough, 2017) xi.

this thought"—he did not, in fact, turn to the topic again. However, he did speak, most often indirectly, of the way in which the church's word gains weight and power not through concepts but by example, of our duty as Christians to attend to the significance of a human example. Exemplification has its origin in the humanity of Jesus and "is so important in Paul's writings!"[119]

I am not a theorist of the genre of biography. I have begun and abandoned many more biographies than I have read to the end, and the ones I finish are often in service to research. But I have wondered, over the years since writing *Strange Glory*, about the relationship of biography and theology. I have wondered why so few theologians write biography.[120] I have wondered whether *theological biography* is a useful moniker and whether the phrase refers to something overt in the life of the subject or to something in the biographer's angle of vision. And does the Christian stand in a different relation to the biography of a saint than in relation to the biography of a more ordinary sinner? (I think all biographers of Bonhoeffer inevitably conclude yes.)

As a reader and a writer, I have been drawn to biography because of my belief that systematic and philosophical theology must be illuminated by biographical and historical realities. That belief seems near creedal for any professor of our decidedly incarnational and historical Christian faith. I can read the piercing meditations of Søren Kierkegaard or Hans Urs von Balthasar on our convulsive existence or the dizziness of freedom as aspects of Christian wisdom and, indeed, as part of life with God—of our anxiety as primordially grounded in God's anxiety toward the world. But beyond those meditations, I also want to know how exactly anxiety was useful to Kierkegaard. How did he experience

119. Bonhoeffer, *Letters and Papers from Prison*, 504 and 561–62.

120. In *Biography as Theology*, James McClendon makes a provisional case for the importance of biography in reading and understanding theological texts. Any theology, he says, that "does not enter into the actual shape of the lives of the people in its community of concern, is after all irrelevant to [our] lives" (McClendon, *Biography as Theology: How Life Stories Can Remake Today's Theology* [Eugene, OR: Wipf & Stock, 2002; first published in 1974 by Abingdon] 21).

anxiety? Solely as a means for overturning the Hegelian dialectic? Or was it something he struggled with, fought, or welcomed? How did he feel it in his body? Truth claims and assertions about God are not eliminated by idiosyncratic details of the self; they are instantiated.

On my shelf of favorite biographies is not much that could be considered theological, if by that modifier we mean subjects or biographers explicitly interested in theology. Instead, there are biographies of Robert Lowell, Virginia Woolf, Samuel Beckett, and Simone de Beauvoir. More recently, I added Marshall Frady's biography of George Wallace and Masha Gessen's biography of Vladimir Putin. What makes for good biography has little to do, it seems to me, with theology. Good biography feels rather like a novel in its attention to language, in its insistence on capturing the seams of life, in its devotion to atmosphere and color—see, for example, Taylor Branch's evocation of jubilant mass meetings and dark Alabama nights in his *Parting the Waters*. And good biography, like good fiction, can give readers the material to develop judgments that the author does not make. The reader has first the biographer's account, but she's also given the material to shape her own portrait—for example, to detect in Walker Percy's biography signs of self-pity and paternalism where the biographer may see a white liberal ardor.[121]

The dearth of beautiful biographies of people of faith is lamentable. A marvelous exception is Clare Carlisle's *Philosopher of the Heart*, which is as wise and artful as any book I've read in years. Another is Gregory Alan Thornbury's revelatory portrait of Larry Norman.[122]

---

121. Frady, *Wallace* (New York: Random House, 1975); Gessen, *The Man Without a Face: The Unlikely Rise of Vladimir Putin* (New York: Penguin, 2012); Branch, *Parting the Waters: America in the King Years 1954–1963* (New York: Simon & Schuster, 1988); Bertram Wyatt-Brown, *The House of Percy: Honor, Melancholy, and Imagination in a Southern Family* (New York: Oxford University Press, 1994).

122. Carlisle, *Philosopher of the Heart: The Restless Life of Søren Kierkegaard* (New York: Farrar, Straus & Giroux, 2019); and Thornbury, *Why Should the Devil Have All the Good Music? Larry Norman and the Perils of Christian*

In my evangelical adolescence, I read biographies of missionaries, evangelists, born-again stoners, and street fighters. As literature, most of them are terrible, and I am drawn intellectually to life stories that probe the literary excellences, capture the vital spark of character. At the same time, the books I read as a teenager—especially those in the drugs-to-Jesus canon—may have been badly written, but they were not plodding. They did not lack "ordering force."[123] Every one of them was commended to me for my spiritual edification, not for being works of art.

Perhaps a biography becomes theological only in its impact on the reader. When I read Jay Tolson, what's awakened in me is a sense of compassion for Percy and an awareness of how much suffering goes into art. When I read Lee on Woolf—a book that unsettles me every time I open its pages—that compassion manifests as a desire to be alongside this real and brilliant and fearless and broken person.[124] I find myself wishing I could save her. That desire is much like Marc Pachter's affirmation of the biographer's "near missionary drive" to save a soul or personality for "the company of future generations." Any serious biography represents an author's quest for reconciliation—the effort to make a different life compatible with her own. Reconcilers seek to renew or restore what was lost, to see, in Joan Didion's words, "the sermon in the suicide."[125] So while Christian readers and writers always wrestle with the specter of hagiography, I'll admit that I read and write biography in part because I want to be nourished, edified, strengthened.

So, then, what of the aforementioned biography of George Wallace? What of the biographies of Hitler and his henchmen?

I return again to my Southern Baptist childhood. Before evangelicals became culture warriors, their children were taught

Rock (New York: Convergent, 2018).

123. Reed Whittemore, *Whole Lives: Shapers of Modern Biography* (Baltimore, MD: Johns Hopkins University Press, 1989) 163.

124. Tolson, *Pilgrim in the Ruins: A Life of Walker Percy* (New York: Simon & Schuster, 1992); and Hermione Lee, *Virginia Woolf* (New York: Knopf, 1997).

125. Pachter, "Biographer Himself," 4; and Didion, *We Tell Ourselves Stories in Order to Live: Collected Nonfiction* (New York: Knopf, 2006) 185.

to love. All the ancient words of the faith were spoken over us: new birth in Christ, sanctification and the Holy Spirit, the miracles of the cross and resurrection, brother love, sister love, enemy love. Likewise, biography is a redemptive exercise. To be sure, the telling of a life story runs the risk of justifying atrocity. Yet any moral reader would be obligated to say that the act of understanding the formation of white segregationists is an act of love for the world.

I have often heard biographers say that they became tired of their subject in the course of research and writing. My fascination with Bonhoeffer is greater than when I started the biography nearly a decade ago. Proclaiming the truth of the gospel while pondering the end of Christianity, plotting the assassination of Hitler while affirming the ethics of pacifism, celebrating the sacrament of marriage while binding his affections joyfully to another man—Bonhoeffer came to embody some of the perplexing contradictions that modernity imposed upon the faith. I could happily pass the rest of my life sorting through these intricacies of character and belief.

So let's give Bonhoeffer the last word.

Going into the depths of the human condition with as much honesty as one can muster is, for Bonhoeffer, the most reliable guide to understanding humanity created in the image of God. Discipleship is the cross-marked way to consummate humanism—and so, as Bonhoeffer wrote in his final meditations on the worldliness of Christian faith and practice, we dare not confess the resurrection of the dead until we have found a way, with all our hearts, to love the earth in all its sufferings. And thus, we write biography.[126]

126. I am grateful to the many people who read drafts of this ever-expanding work and especially to those who helped bring it to the finish line: Theresa Clasen in Berlin, Germany; Isaac Barnes May in Charlottesville, Virginia; and Lauren Winner, in Durham, North Carolina. I also wish to thank the exceedingly patient editors at *The Other Journal*, Dan Rhodes and Zac Settle, as well as Andrew Shutes-David, the best copy editor with whom I've ever worked.

INDEX

Index

Made in the USA
Columbia, SC
25 February 2023

12976314R00048